PRAISE

ELEVATE

"This text is coming at the appropriate time as an unrelenting global pandemic continues to plague our educational institutions and our students continually toggle between remote and in-class learning, which can cause frustration and instability. As appropriately titled, this book will elevate the mindsets of students to be resilient and to know that they can persist through circumstances while learning simultaneously. Dr. Perryman and Mrs. Perryman have seamlessly interwoven excitement, academic support, and child development activities into one book. Thus, the authors have created a curriculum that will inspire the next generations of leaders to continue to elevate, innovate, create, and make our world a better, safer place."

Dr. Erik M. Hines, PhD
Associate Professor
Florida State University College of Education

"Dr. and Mrs. Perryman provide a phenomenal tool to improve youth development and empowerment through a structured system of encouragement, inspiration, and affirmation. Additionally, the ELEVATE! curriculum will lead to a greater level of positive language literacy that will undoubtedly encourage youth to use positive and supportive language more often in their daily lives."

Dr. Ed-Dee G. Williams, MSW, PhD
Postdoctoral Fellow, University of Michigan School of Social Work
Assistant Professor, Boston College School of Social Work

"For the past five years, Hatchuel Tabernik & Associates has been honored to be the evaluators for the Center of Hope's out-of-school-time program, ELEVATE! The program serves about 150 children and their families five days per week during the school year and for six weeks during the summer each year. Dr. Perryman has designed this culturally affirmative program to center on equity.

"The vast majority of children served by ELEVATE! are from families of color living in or near poverty. The program promotes healthy, successful children by helping them develop a growth mindset and enhance their social skills.

"The program engages parents and guardians in activities that help them support their children's education and their family's advancement. All of the parents surveyed rated the program as excellent."

Tim Tabernik
Hatchuel Tabernik & Associates

ELEVATE

TRACEE PERRYMAN, PHD & WILLETTA PERRYMAN

ELEVATE

AN AFTERSCHOOL ENRICHMENT MODEL FOR FOSTERING CHILDREN'S ACADEMIC, SOCIAL, AND EMOTIONAL RESILIENCE

Advantage

Published by Advantage, Charleston, South Carolina.
Member of Advantage Media Group.

ADVANTAGE is a registered trademark, and the Advantage colophon is a trademark of Advantage Media Group, Inc.

Printed in the United States of America.

10 9 8 7 6 5 4 3 2 1

ISBN: 978-1-64225-355-9
LCCN: 2022902719

Cover design by David Taylor.
Layout design by Wesley Strickland.

This publication is designed to provide accurate and authoritative information in regard to the subject matter covered. It is sold with the understanding that the publisher is not engaged in rendering legal, accounting, or other professional services. If legal advice or other expert assistance is required, the services of a competent professional person should be sought.

 Advantage Media Group is proud to be a part of the Tree Neutral® program. Tree Neutral offsets the number of trees consumed in the production and printing of this book by taking proactive steps such as planting trees in direct proportion to the number of trees used to print books. To learn more about Tree Neutral, please visit **www.treeneutral.com**.

Advantage Media Group is a publisher of business, self-improvement, and professional development books and online learning. We help entrepreneurs, business leaders, and professionals share their Stories, Passion, and Knowledge to help others Learn & Grow. Do you have a manuscript or book idea that you would like us to consider for publishing? Please visit **advantagefamily.com**.

To my niece and Willetta's granddaughter, Jamison,
who continues to be an inspiration. Every day, we work to
ensure that ELEVATE! is a place where we would be excited to
send her. And to all of the ELEVATE! students and families we
have served over decades. As we teach them, they teach us.

CONTENTS

FOREWORD

ONE OF MY FAVORITE educators, Dr. Carter G. Woodson, said, "Real education means to inspire people to live more abundantly, to learn to begin with life as they find it and make it better." I believe an education gives children an opportunity to explore the world, to get inspired to make a positive impact, and to develop the inquisitiveness to be innovative to advance our society. Moreover, I believe educators can be the facilitators of inspiring kids to be the next generation of innovators, entrepreneurs, doctors, beauticians, barbers, and lawyers. However, educators must ensure that *all* students regardless of race, disability, gender, religion, and age have access to education that inspires them to make scalable impact in our society.

In their book, *ELEVATE: An Afterschool Enrichment Model for Fostering Children's Academic, Social, and Emotional Resilience*, Dr. Perryman and Mrs. Perryman provide lesson plans to achieve what Dr. Woodson saw as the purpose of education: inspiration. Further, the authors provide academic learning tools that coincide with building student character and confidence. I believe Dr. Perryman and Mrs. Perryman have developed a text where children can connect what they learn to their personal lives. Making education relatable to the lives of students is a great recipe for high levels of engagement. I like how the authors have students repeat affirmations, participate in circle time, learn vocabulary related to the lesson, sing, and participate in arts and crafts. Additionally, the lessons are connected to Common Core standards.

This text is coming at the appropriate time as an unrelenting global pandemic continues to plague our educational institutions and our students continually toggle between remote and in-class learning, which can cause frustration and instability. As appropriately titled, this book will elevate the mindsets of students to be resilient and to know that they can persist through circumstances while simultaneously learning. Dr. Perryman and Mrs. Perryman have seamlessly interwoven excitement, academic support, and child development activities into one book.

It is clear the authors are dedicated to making a curriculum that is backed by education standards, culturally relevant, and aimed at reducing opportunity gaps, specifically around academic achievement. Further, creating a curriculum designed for afterschool programs provides the additional support needed for students who may not receive it during traditional school hours. Also, Dr. Perryman and Mrs. Perryman are experts in this area given their vast experiences in K-12 education, higher education, and government agencies.

Education provides the tools needed for students to be prepared for any postsecondary opportunities including college, the armed forces, vocational/technical school, and the world of work. Plus, it has provided our society the ingenuity to develop space travel for private citizens, cars that run completely on electricity, and the ability to use video conference tools to work anywhere in the world.

Thus, the authors have created a curriculum that will inspire the next generations of leaders to continue to elevate, innovate, create, and make our world a better, safer place.

ERIK M. HINES
Associate Professor, Florida State University
emhines@fsu.edu

AN INTRODUCTION TO ELEVATE!

What Is ELEVATE?

ELEVATE! is a comprehensive twenty-eight-week after-school curriculum for fostering academic, emotional, and social resilience in children from kindergarten through third grade. The curriculum can also be adapted for older children. The program supports students from a variety of backgrounds to elevate their lives, helping them

- develop leadership skills for greater empowerment,

- strengthen identity and character development,

- increase engagement in education through enrichment activities,

- improve literacy and reading skills,

- increase confidence and self-direction,

1

- cultivate cooperation and community, and

- learn life skills.

The ELEVATE! Framework

ELEVATE! honors and seeks to restore a child's cultural identity and expand opportunity for children living in urban and suburban communities. The framework for our curriculum is built upon a rich legacy of cultural stories and solid, evidence-based academic research.

The ELEVATE! curriculum has been enriched by three streams of research and practice: the foundational principles of values-based approaches from a variety of cultures, best practices for after-school programs informed by positive youth development theory, and the principles of Culturally Relevant Pedagogy. For a fuller discussion of background influences and the academic research that provide the foundation for the curriculum, see the book *Elevating Futures: A Model for Empowering Black Elementary Student Success* by Tracee Perryman, PhD.

Four Pillars of ELEVATE!

ELEVATE! provides a safe, nurturing environment for children to learn and grow. Delivered over seven or nine months, the curriculum is based on four pillars:

- Academic excellence

- Educational enrichment

- Positive youth development

- Family/parent/community engagement

Key Benefits of ELEVATE!

In addition to a commitment to cultivate academic resilience with a focus on math and literacy skill development, ELEVATE! offers children the following key benefits:

- Positive learning environment

- Social and emotional development

- Arts enrichment

- Health and recreation

What Makes ELEVATE! Exceptional?

The ELEVATE! curriculum was born out of an award-winning program in northwest Ohio that has been recognized for excellence and innovation. The Center of Hope Family Services Inc. (CHFS) has shepherded the curriculum during its early years. A recipient of the national Nonprofit Innovation and Excellence Awards, CHFS also received the 21st Century Community Learning Center Award for Academic Improvement in reading and literacy from the Ohio Department of Education in 2018.

Today ELEVATE! is available for use in after-school and community settings nationwide. The vision is to broadly share the ELEVATE! difference to improve the lives of children and families in communities across the United States and beyond. The curriculum is distinct from other after-school curricula designed for children in the following ways:

- Proven results in academic performance and attendance

- Collaboration among teachers, volunteers, parents, and the community

- Creativity and a fun learning environment that engages children

- A love-based approach that provides a safe and nurturing learning environment

ELEVATE! Student Outcomes

ELEVATE! closes the achievement gap and ensures equity of opportunity for students in urban and suburban communities through

- development of a positive sense of self,

- affirming the identity of a variety of racial groups,

- high expectations for achievement,

- self-efficacy to excel, and

- motivation to elevate and be elevated by their community.

We believe all children are gifted, capable of learning, and capable of succeeding academically and socially. Practitioners simply need to be equipped with the proper tools to facilitate their learning and success. The ELEVATE! curriculum is specifically designed to support children from diverse backgrounds in developing key social, educational, and emotional skills. Outcomes include

- improvements in grade-level performance in reading, language arts, and math;

- increased school attendance;

- better mental and emotional well-being;

- improved problem-solving skill; and

- higher levels of parental involvement and engagement.

The ELEVATE! Difference: Results

Center of Hope started a five-week summer pilot program in June of 2021, serving students from Sylvania public schools. For many students, this was the most meaningful in-person integration they had experienced since the start of COVID.

After five weeks of instruction, we achieved the following results:

- 53 percent were working at a higher reading level than that at which they started (e.g., moving up from mid-K to late K, mid-3 to early 4, etc.). Therefore, 53 percent of students demonstrated improvements in reading.

- 76 percent of students were working at a higher math level than that at which they started (e.g., moving up from mid-K to late K, mid-3 to early 4, etc.). Therefore, 76 percent of students demonstrated improvements in math.

- 70 percent of parents and 75 percent of students reported gains in social and emotional skills over the course of the five-week programs.

Students enrolled in ELEVATE! after-school programs at three schools in Toledo, Ohio, showed marked improvements in reading and math test scores and attendance. Parents and program staff reported significant improvements in overall well-being as well as behavioral adjustments.

"The children are excited to come to ELEVATE! every day, and you can tell that they are learning to be better students" (ELEVATE! employee).

2019–2020 RESULTS

During the 2019–2020 school year at Martin Luther King Jr. Elementary School, ELEVATE! students

- showed an improvement in their reading grade point average,

- showed an improvement in their math grade point average,

- demonstrated an increase in their school day attendance, and

- reduced their total number of unexcused absence hours.

During the 2019–2020 school year at Old West End Elementary School, ELEVATE! students

- showed an improvement in their English/language arts grade point average,

- showed significant increases in school day attendance rate,

- decreased their rate of chronic absenteeism, and

- achieved an 89 percent after-school program attendance rate.

During the 2019–2020 school year at Robinson Elementary School, ELEVATE! students

- showed an improvement in their reading grade point average,

- maintained an excellent school day attendance rate, and

- reduced their total number of unexcused absence hours.

2018–19 RESULTS

During the 2018–2019 school year at Martin Luther King Jr. Elementary School,

- 100 percent of regular attendees scored proficient or above on the Ohio Computer Based Assessment (OCBA) in math in 2019;

- 100 percent of parents reported that the ELEVATE! program helped their child(ren) at least somewhat with getting along with other students, and 91 percent reported that it helped very much;

- 100 percent of parents agreed that the ELEVATE! program staff cared about their child(ren) and wanted to see them succeed;

- 100 percent of staff reported that the ELEVATE! program helped students at least somewhat with social skills and interacting with others;

- 84 percent of participants scored on or above grade level on the Edmentum math diagnostic test;

- 32 percent of participants scored on or above grade level on the Edmentum reading diagnostic test at the start of the year, and 60 percent scored on or above grade level at the end of the year; and

- school disciplinary actions decreased between 2017–18 and 2018–19 for regular attendees, suggesting improved student behavior.

During the 2018–2019 school year at Old West End Elementary School,

- 75 percent of participants scored on or above grade level on the Edmentum math diagnostic test,

- scores for the Edmentum reading diagnostic test increased from 45 percent at the beginning of the year to 64 percent at the end of the year, and

- ELEVATE! students achieved a 97 percent after-school program attendance rate.

The ELEVATE! Difference: Collaboration

At the heart of ELEVATE! is a collaborative approach that sets our curriculum apart from other after-school curricula. Instructors work closely with students and engage volunteers, parents, family members, and the larger community. Monthly family activities and quarterly stakeholder engagement activities further expand and enrich the lives of children, their families, and the communities they call home. All participants come together to ELEVATE! and rally around to provide resources to children and their families. This emphasis on collaboration and community partnership has supported the achievement of a 97 percent success rate at a cost of just $5,354 per student compared with an estimated cost per nonintervention of more than three times that rate at $16,461.

The ELEVATE! Difference: Creativity

Creativity is the crux of the ELEVATE! curriculum, which integrates both visual and performing arts and makes learning fun. Unlike traditional educational curricula, ELEVATE! engages children through creative expression and learning activities that reinforce key educational concepts, engaging all the senses and supporting social and emotional development alongside the proficiency in core educational concepts.

> "Often the children are learning, but they don't know that they're learning. ELEVATE! makes learning fun" (Willetta Perryman).

"Often the children are learning, but they don't know that they're learning. ELEVATE! makes learning fun" (Willetta Perryman).

The ELEVATE! Difference: Love

Love truly is at the core of ELEVATE! Unlike purely academic programs, ELEVATE! is rooted in a holistic approach that considers all aspects of child development and thriving individually and in community. With a commitment to collective development and the value of harmony, the curriculum is well rounded with a balance of both individual and group learning activities. ELEVATE! includes an awareness of the trauma some children have faced in their communities. A focus on reversing the damage resulting from structural disadvantage and overt racism is woven throughout the curriculum.

"This program is based on love. ELEVATE! uplifts children and instills positive character development" (ELEVATE! employee).

Meet the Creators of ELEVATE!

TRACEE PERRYMAN, PHD

Dr. Tracee Perryman is cofounder and CEO of Center of Hope Family Services. She graduated with honors from the University of Michigan, where she majored in psychology. She earned a master's degree in mental health counseling from Bowling Green State University, where she supervised students majoring in early childhood education. Dr. Perryman then earned her PhD, with a minor in education, from the Ohio State University College of Social Work. She was awarded a fellowship from Goldman Sachs, where she earned a certificate in small business management.

Dr. Perryman is a recognized expert in getting results for underserved individuals and families through data-driven, evidence-based interventions that are culturally relevant. She worked with an independent evaluation firm to conduct a social return on investment for the programs she designed for Center of Hope Family Services. Findings revealed that CHFS generates six dollars in community savings for every one dollar invested. Dr. Perryman's successes have established her as a thought leader in developing *programs that work* for underserved individuals.

Dr. Perryman has applied her studies in psychology, mental health, social work, and education to co-develop, with Willetta Perryman, the innovative after-school curriculum that is now known as ELEVATE! Known to the children, families, and communities she inspires as "Doctor P," Dr. Perryman has provided consultation and training workshops to governmental agencies, national and regional foundations, and nonprofit agencies in the following areas:

- High-quality program development and implementation
- Culturally relevant program development and implementation
- Youth development best practices
- Development of sustainable program processes
- Data collection analysis and reporting systems development
- Family engagement in youth development programming
- Family engagement in juvenile justice system reform

Connect and learn more at https://doctor-p.com.

WILLETTA PERRYMAN

Mrs. Willetta Perryman is cofounder and chief program officer (CPO) of Center of Hope Family Services. She majored in early childhood education at the University of Toledo and served for fifteen years as an early learning educator. She founded the Creative Village Child Development Center, rated by the Ohio Department of Education as a high-quality center and model program for centers statewide. Creative Village quickly became a 21st Century Community Learning Center and is now called ELEVATE! Overseeing every aspect of the program at the Martin Luther King School for Boys, she helped quadruple the number of students reading at grade level and reduce school suspension rates from 32 percent to just 6 percent.

Willetta Perryman has always emphasized the importance of family engagement in youth programming. She was the driving force behind the Center of Hope Family Navigator program, inspiring parents to cope more effectively and become leaders in their families and communities. Willetta has consulted on the reading and visual arts components of the ELEVATE! curriculum, and she is the author of the ELEVATE! Cooking Up Hope family engagement curriculum, which infuses cooking with tangible strategies for developing healthy, well-adjusted children. The program was featured in the Toledo Blade newspaper in November 2020.

With a proven track record of identifying key benchmarks that students may have missed in the early years of their formative education, she has designed and implemented a variety of innovative solutions to equip these students to perform at grade level or above through her impressive career as an educator. She has also developed strategies to engage and motivate students to learn and grow socially and emotionally. Many of these strategies have become the bedrock foundation of the ELEVATE! curriculum.

Willetta served as an educator for Toledo Head Start, where she became well respected for the innovative cultural, visual, and performing arts programs she brought to the classroom and to parent engagement. During her tenure, she earned the child development associate credential. Willetta has also developed a women's empowerment curriculum for faith-based organizations and shared strategies for churches to educate for activism. She is married to Dr. Donald Perryman.

GUIDELINES FOR IMPLEMENTATION

The ELEVATE! Curriculum

The ELEVATE! curriculum provides detailed lesson plans based on designated themes that cover seven to nine months of teaching opportunities. From a social development standpoint, the lesson plans provide teachers a road map to engage children's feelings, to teach children how to lift themselves and each other up, and to build community and harmony while providing continual motivation through music and affirmations.

- The ELEVATE! curriculum is a progressive, holistic after-school curriculum that begins with individual identity and an affirmation of confidence.

- We then move beyond the individual, establishing a sense of family and togetherness, building our circle.

- From there, we tackle what harmony and family look like and how each individual participates in their community through cooperation.

- Now the children are ready to learn how to use their skills and talents to contribute to their community and the world.

- Next, we embrace expression and explore the ways we can use our creativity to find and fulfill our purpose.

- Then we elevate our future.

- Finally, we embrace hope for a better tomorrow.

The ELEVATE! curriculum empowers teachers to move beyond compliance and to engage students instead through genuine, culturally relevant engagement. Most importantly, the curriculum gives children a real voice in their achievement and success. When a child has agency in their learning, the child will no longer participate just because they are required to; instead, they will participate because they want to be a part of the learning community.

The Seven ELEVATE! Themes

ELEVATE! supports families and the communities they call home by helping children elevate their lives. Each of these seven-unit themes is explored in depth over the course of a month. Through a flexible weekly curriculum typically delivered in an after-school setting, children learn about

1. Elevating Confidence,

2. Elevating Our Circle,

3. Elevating Cooperation,

4.   Elevating Community,

5.   Elevating Expression,

6.   Elevating into Our Future, and

7.   Elevating Hope.

ELEVATE!'s Six Tenets

Each unit/theme is brought to life through the outlined methods below.

1. WE SHINE TOGETHER

- Each lesson will begin with the "ELEVATE! Affirmation" song, whose lyrics are listed at the beginning of each lesson for ease of use.

- The plan will include daily affirmations:
  "Today I feel _____
  _____
  _____";
  "I can make my day better by _____
  _____
  _____";
  "I can help make _____'s day better by
  _____
  _____."

- Shining Together: Each lesson will include instructions to recognize specific students for their daily academic and social accomplishments.

2. WE LEARN TOGETHER

- The curriculum will include an introduction of each new theme.

- The curriculum will be divided into specific lessons targeted to the theme.

- Each lesson will highlight real people and real issues students will encounter every day in the news, in their homes, in their communities.

- The focus will be on reading and cooperative activities.

- The curriculum will feature easy-to-read illustrated books available online featuring Black characters and questions created to measure understanding and engage students more fully with the story.

- The curriculum will introduce key concepts accompanied by questions to engage students and provide opportunities for them to apply new knowledge.

- Guidelines will be provided to support students at varying levels of reading ability.

3. WE GROW TOGETHER

- Discussion questions will connect key concepts from the book to contemporary issues students may encounter in their homes and communities.

4. WE STRIVE TOGETHER

- Lesson plans will include specific, age- and grade-level goals and objectives that align with Common Core standards.

- Lesson plans will include general vocabulary from the reading selections.

- Lesson plans will include ELEVATE! Wise Words, vocabulary connected to the reading lesson designed to build language skills.

5. WE WORK TOGETHER

- Each lesson will include art/craft projects specific to the unit, allowing students to grow through individual expression and grow in their public speaking confidence through presentations.

6. WE RISE TOGETHER

- A recap of key learning points will provide opportunities for students to practice and increase skills independently.

- Each lesson will conclude with an ELEVATE! superstar chant:

  - [Child's name, group name, or the entire class] is a superstar.

  - [Child's achievement] makes [her/him] a superstar.

  - Keep shooting for the stars.

  - We love to watch you *elevate*!

ELEVATE!: The Key to Success Is You!

We believe that the teacher or instructor is the key component to the implementation of any curriculum. The ELEVATE! curriculum, no matter how robust and impactful, can only truly be effective if the teacher or practitioner fully believes the following:

- All children are capable of learning.

- All children can succeed academically.

- Achievement gaps can be narrowed and even closed.

- Urban children are deserving of the same time, commitment, and resources as their nonurban counterparts.

Do you believe? Are you ready to instill that belief in your students?

ELEVATE! Class Size/ Learning Pods

- A one-to-ten or one-to-twelve teacher to student ratio works best.

- Break out into learning pods or small groups for reading.

- Group children by age and grade for reading activities.

ELEVATE! Weekday Focus Suggestions

If your program, class, or group meets three days each week, we suggest you highlight the following activities for each weekly lesson:

- DAY 1 — "ELEVATE! Affirmation" song, overview, and beginning discussion

- DAY 2 — "ELEVATE! Affirmation" song and recommended reading

- DAY 3 — "ELEVATE! Affirmation" song and arts and crafts activity

If your program, class, or group meets five days each week, we suggest you follow this more robust schedule using this curriculum guide:

- DAY 1 — "ELEVATE Affirmation" song, overview, and discussion.

- DAY 2 — "ELEVATE! Affirmation" song and recommended reading.

- DAY 3 — "ELEVATE! Affirmation" song and arts and crafts activity.

- DAY 4 — "ELEVATE! Affirmation" song and homework help—bring in community partners to provide performing arts enrichment or STEM-based activities. These kinds of partners can be found at the university setting. Partners can also use computer-based tutoring tools. i-Ready, Success-Maker, and Edmentum are a few resources.

- DAY 5 — ELEVATE! "Affirmation" song, community guests, and recreation—community partners are simply individuals in the community who can come in as guest speakers, mentors, etc. Speak to organized recreation and intramural leagues, where children are taught different cooperative team sports, which give them the opportunity to work together while also instilling recreation and fitness.

ELEVATE! Preparation

To prepare for delivering the ELEVATE! curriculum in your after-school or classroom environment, you will want to prepare your staff and volunteers and your environment. Here are a few tips to set your ELEVATE! classroom up for success.

Create a Positive Learning Environment

It's important to create a welcoming environment for children. Decorate your space with inspiring posters, quotes, and affirmations to connect students to ELEVATE! values. Have an open space where children can sit on the floor with pillows or at tables. Place craft supplies in one area of the room. Designate an area for ELEVATE! books and instructional materials.

Set Up for Teaching Success

Ensure your instructional area is equipped with a whiteboard or screen where you can write key points. Meet with your instructional team of teachers and volunteers to discuss how you will place students into grade-level groups, usually one group for kindergarten and first graders and another group for second- and third-grade students. If possible, decide in advance which teacher or volunteer will work with each group.

Purchase Books

We suggest you preorder recommended books, which are accessible online. If your budget allows, purchase books for the children in your classroom. At a minimum, you will need a few copies of each book.

Gather Supplies

Stock your classroom with supplies for arts and crafts items. We recommend having an ample supply of the following on hand: glue sticks or glue, scissors for children, multicolored poster board, construction paper, and decorative items that can be affixed to paper, such as feathers, colored gemstones, and stickers. Some arts and crafts sessions will require additional supplies, such as inexpensive T-shirts or other items you can find at your local or online craft store. Have music selections prepared for play before each lesson.

Weekly Preparation

At the end of each lesson, you will find notes for preparation for the week ahead. All instructors should be familiar with the lesson materials and have invested adequate time for full preparation.

ELEVATE! Music

The ELEVATE! curriculum includes a variety of musical selections especially designed to motivate students and create an optimal learning environment for children. Song selections help affirm children and create a sense of community in your classroom.

Following is a list of songs and the corresponding units in which you will want to share these songs. We suggest you plan the songs before class, as students are arriving and moving to their designated classroom seats or gathering spots, and as students are engaged in activities, such as the arts and crafts portion of each lesson.

ELEVATE! Musical Selections

UNIT 1

→ "ELEVATE!" (before class)

→ "ELEVATE! Affirmation"

→ "ELEVATE! Superstars"

UNIT 2

→ "ELEVATE!" (before class)

→ "ELEVATE! Affirmation"

→ "ELEVATE! Superstars"

→ "Children of Royalty" (during activities)

UNIT 3

→ "ELEVATE!" (before class)

→ "Children of Royalty" (before class)ˈ

→ "ELEVATE! Affirmation"

→ "ELEVATE! Superstars"

→ "When I Win, We Win" (during activities)

UNIT 4

→ "ELEVATE!" (before class)

→ "ELEVATE! Affirmation"

→ "ELEVATE! Superstars"

➡ "Children of Royalty" (during activities)

➡ "When I Win, We Win" (during activities)

UNIT 5

➡ "ELEVATE!" (before class)

➡ "Children of Royalty" (before class)

➡ "When I Win, We Win" (before class)

➡ "ELEVATE! Affirmation"

➡ "ELEVATE! Superstars"

➡ "Watch Me ELEVATE!" (during activities)

UNIT 6

➡ "ELEVATE!" (before class)

➡ "Children of Royalty" (before class)

➡ "When I Win, We Win" (before class)

➡ "Watch me ELEVATE!" (before class)

➡ "ELEVATE! Affirmation"

➡ "ELEVATE! Superstars"

➡ "It's Our Time" (during activities)

UNIT 7

➡ "ELEVATE!" (before class)

➡ "Children of Royalty" (before class)

➡ "When I Win, We Win" (before class)

- "Watch me ELEVATE!" (before class)

- "ELEVATE! Affirmation"

- "ELEVATE! Superstars"

- "Elevating Hope" (during activities)

- "It's Our Time" (during activities)

ELEVATE! Virtual Delivery

ELEVATE! can be adapted for delivery to students virtually using videoconferencing technology or through prerecorded video units. This was done successfully in 2020, and we encourage after-school programs working with children at home due to health-related restrictions and other factors to adapt lesson plans for online delivery.

DAILY PLAN

Daily check-ins, followed by the ELEVATE! affirmations and the "ELEVATE!" song, are recommended at a minimum, though other lesson material can be easily adapted for sharing in a virtual classroom. Adapt other lesson content as time allows. Consider providing incentives for children who participate in the virtual classroom.

PREPARATION

Before delivering weekly content virtually, read the entire unit and each lesson plan thoroughly. Gather all materials (books, supplies, recordings of songs, and demonstration materials) and have them easily accessible when delivering content. Remember to include step-by-step instructions for students during your presentation. If you plan on sharing vocabulary words on screen, type these into a presentation in advance.

ABOUT TECHNOLOGY

Sharing the curriculum online must be done through a secure channel that is not publicly accessible. For example, you may not publish videos to YouTube. We recommend password-protected content to ensure only your students and families can access the material. Do a technology check before the scheduled connection time and create a connection checklist. Provide connection guidelines to parents and children.

SUPPLY PACKETS

Think through how you will get supplies to children in advance. One option is to deliver a weekly or monthly packet to children at home or have parents or caregivers pick these up at a centralized location. This packet might include:

- items needed for arts and crafts,

- adapted instructions as needed, and

- a red, green, and yellow card for voting.*

*Alternatively, you can encourage children to signal their votes with a thumbs-up, a thumbs-down, or a thumb to the side.

ELEVATE! Parent Engagement

Parent and family engagement is a vital part of the ELEVATE! approach. The family component further enriches the lessons that children are encountering through the core curriculum. At the beginning of each unit, we will include tips for engaging parents and families as well as the

Parent and family engagement is a vital part of the ELEVATE! approach.

broader network of support for children in schools and community organizations.

We anticipate making a special ELEVATE! curriculum for parents and families available in the future. Until this complementary curriculum product is available, we recommend that teachers actively engage parents and caretakers, encouraging them to support the child's learning and growth around the theme for each unit.

ELEVATE! License to Use

Know that the ELEVATE! curriculum is protected by US copyright and may only be incorporated into your after-school or community program with a license to use. Materials are only to be used by those who have purchased a license.

ELEVATE! Acknowledgments

Definitions used throughout the curriculum are from the Merriam-Webster Online Dictionary website here: https://www.merriam-webster.com. Links mentioned in this section are accurate as of the time of publication.

ELEVATE! OVERVIEW

THE ELEVATE! CURRICULUM is designed to be presented weekly, with one lesson plan for each week and four lessons for each of the seven units. The twenty-eight-week curriculum can be delivered over a seven-month or nine-month period. It may also be adapted for after-school programs that do not meet every day or for online use. The following pages include a welcome and introduction to ELEVATE! for your students.

As students gather for the first time, let's begin with an introduction to ELEVATE! In this overview lesson, you will lead students in a discussion of what it means to be an ELEVATE! scholar, the ELEVATE! essentials, and how we will elevate in our journey together throughout the year.

Welcome students and affirm them as they enter the classroom. Share any classroom guidelines or routines (where students should place backpacks and jackets, where they should sit, etc.).

What Does It Mean to Be an ELEVATE! Scholar?

Lead the children in a discussion about what it means to elevate. Start by talking about the word *elevate* itself. Ask, "Does anyone know the meaning of the word *elevate*?"

Invite the children to share their ideas first. Then read the definition below from the Merriam-Webster Online Dictionary (https://www.merriam-webster.com).

➡ to lift or make higher: *raise*
  • elevate a patient's leg, exercises that elevate the heart rate

➡ to raise in rank or status
  • was elevated to chairperson

➡ to improve morally, intellectually, or culturally
  • great books that both entertain and elevate their readers

➡ to raise the spirits of: *elate*

Say, "An ELEVATE! scholar is committed to learning and growing and to rising in the world. We're going to explore many ways we can elevate together!"

ELEVATE! Essentials

Say, "At ELEVATE! there are four things we know are true about each and every person in this room. Can you guess what they are?" Allow the children to offer responses and express themselves. Engage in dialogue to set a tone for learning and growth in an environment where all perspectives are honored. Offer encouragement to the children as they participate in the conversation.

After about five minutes of discussion, ask, "Are you ready for me to reveal what it means to be an ELEVATE! scholar?" Pause for a response. Then with enthusiasm and connection to each quality and to the students gathered, share each of the following statements.

- You are great! I am great. I choose to elevate!

- You are unique! I am unique. I choose to elevate!

- You have special talents! I have special talents. I choose to elevate!

- You will always try to do your best! I will do my best. I choose to elevate!

Once you have shared each quality, invite students to repeat it with you, replacing the words *you are*, *you have*, and *you will* with *I am*, *I have*, and *I will*. Have the students repeat the phrase with you and follow each statement with "I choose to elevate!"

The **ELEVATE!** Express
This Is How We Elevate!

LEARN

WORK

STRIVE

GROW

SHINE

RISE

FUN

Elevate!

This Is How We *Elevate!*

Say, "So how will we choose to elevate? Here's how we elevate together this year [month, semester]. We take the ELEVATE! Express. We shine together. We learn together. We grow together. We strive together. We work together. We rise together."

We shine together.
We learn together.
We grow together.
We strive together.
We work together.
We rise together.

If you have printed the poster on the previous page, point it out to the children or let them know where they can look in the classroom to remind themselves of the ELEVATE! Express. If time permits, you can talk about each of these words and share with students when you gather the following week that these are the things you will do together each day. You may have the students repeat each of the words after you or invite students to share what each word means to them.

Say, "These are the ways we *elevate!*"

ELEVATE! Express

Say, "There's one more thing that happens when we take the ELEVATE! Express. Does anyone have a guess?"

Allow a few moments for participation. Then say, "When we're all aboard the ELEVATE! Express, we *have fun together!* So are you ready? Let's *elevate!*"

Have the children shout out together, "Let's elevate!"

Say, "When we choose to elevate, we grow higher and higher!"

Say, "So now we've talked about what it means to be an ELEVATE! scholar, and we've talked about the ELEVATE! *Express*—how we will shine, learn, grow, work, strive, and rise together. We also talked about the four ELEVATE! *essentials*. Now let's talk about the third ELEVATE! *E*, which stands for ELEVATE! *expectations*."

What We Expect at ELEVATE!

ELEVATE! EXPECTATIONS

Say, "When we gather to elevate together, there are four things we *expect* from every participant. The first word to remember is *respect*. Can you repeat that with me?"

Ask, "Who can help us understand what *respect* means?" Pause for interaction. "Can someone give me an example of practicing respect?"

- Be respectful.

- Be present.

- Be kind.

- Be open to new ideas.

Move through the other three words in a similar manner, taking a few moments to ask students if they can provide an example for each of the four expectations.

If you have more time for the introduction to ELEVATE! or are spending a full session on the introduction, expand your discussion and include optional activities around the ELEVATE! essentials, ELEVATE! Express, and ELEVATE! expectations.

If you are combining this introduction with lesson 1, move on to lesson 1.

If you are concluding for the day, give students instructions and play the "ELEVATE! Superstars" song and say, "Keep shooting for the stars, ELEVATE! superstars. We love to watch you elevate!"

Provide further direction for students as suits your after-school program.

ELEVATING CONFIDENCE

ELEVATE! Focus:
Elevating Confidence

You are enough! You are worthy and deserving. When we believe in ourselves, we elevate.

ELEVATE! Objective:
Demonstrate Confidence

Students will identify themselves as worthy and deserving, understanding the connection between belief in oneself and the ability to elevate themselves and those around them. Over time, students will consistently self-identify as worthy of living their best lives. They will increasingly make choices and take positive actions to do so.

ELEVATE! Reading: Books for Elevating Confidence

➡ *I Like Myself!* by Karen Beaumont and David Catrow

➡ *A Boy Like You* by Frank Murphy and Kayla Harren

➡ *Superheroes Are Everywhere* by Kamala Harris and Mechal Renee Roe

➡ *Big Plans* by Bob Shea and Lane Smith

ELEVATE! Family Support: Elevating Confidence

Support the child's experience during this unit of ELEVATE! through encouraging and affirming conversations that focus on confidence. Notice each child's level of self-identification as a person of worth and awareness that he or she is deserving of success. Speak words of positive affirmation and belief to your students and encourage them to believe in themselves.

LESSON 1: ELEVATING MY CONFIDENCE

We Shine Together

Say, "Welcome, everyone! Are we ready to *elevate*?" Encourage the children to respond actively and with enthusiasm.

Ask the three daily questions in the ELEVATE! Affirmations section below. You may wish to call on children or simply post the question to the whole group and wait for responses. Invite the children to use their imagination to try new ways to elevate their day and the experience of their classmates.

ELEVATE! AFFIRMATIONS

"Today I feel _____

_____

_____."

"I can make my day better by _____

_____

_____."

"I can help make _____'s day

better by _____

_____

_____."

Remind the children that it's OK to begin where they are. Say, "No matter what kind of day you're having, who you are and how you are is just fine because, together, we can ..." Wait for the children to respond with "*Elevate!*"

Say, "Together, we can elevate! Today we'll talk about how we can elevate our *confidence*. But first, let's do our ELEVATE! affirmations. I'm going to read each affirmation. Then raise your hand if you'd like to share an affirmation today."

Allow three or four responses per question. If time allows, give students time for further reflection and expression, whenever possible focusing on a positive trajectory for their day from here. Ensure that all children are given the opportunity to participate over the course of your after-school program.

"ELEVATE! AFFIRMATION" SONG

Beginning each lesson with the affirmation song allows you, the teacher, to set the cultural tone for the classroom—a tone that tells the students that everyone is welcome and that each and every child will be loved and accepted for their unique traits and abilities. Students can sing along with the recorded version.

Encourage all students to express themselves by singing or participating in a way that feels good to them. You might make instruments available, for example, and encourage children to clap or snap their fingers to keep the rhythm. If you choose, you may also encourage body movements, such as swaying from side to side, dancing creatively, or jumping on the word *elevate*.

Mathematicians and artists,

Musicians and lyricists,

They are all gifts;

They are loved at ELEVATE!

Athletes and readers,

Supporters and leaders,

All kinds of believers

Are loved at ELEVATE!

Hair kinky or straight,

Long tresses or a fade,

Eyes of all shapes

Are loved at ELEVATE!

Fair skin

To every shade of melanin,

We are all kin;

You are loved at ELEVATE!

A temperament that's mild

Or with a little bit of spice,

Personas of all types

Are loved at ELEVATE!

At ELEVATE!

Everybody can find their place;

Never have to worry about feeling hate.

Everybody's loved at ELEVATE!

We Learn Together

ELEVATE! FOCUS

Introduce the theme of this unit—elevating confidence. The ELEVATE! focus in this lesson is "elevating my confidence." Guide the children in a discussion of these themes using the suggested conversation highlights below.

Ask, "What do you think the word *confidence* means?" Invite responses. Discuss the meaning.

CONFIDENCE
/ˈkänfədəns/

1. the feeling or belief that one can rely on someone or something: firm trust.
   - "We had every confidence in the staff."

2. the state of feeling certain about the truth of something.
   - "It is not possible to say with confidence how much of the increase in sea levels is due to melting glaciers."

3. a feeling of self-assurance arising from one's appreciation of one's own abilities or qualities.
   - "She's brimming with confidence."

Ask, "How well do you know who you are?" Invite responses. Probe deeper by asking, "Who do you think you are?"

Say, "Sometimes we may not know who we are simply because we haven't stopped to appreciate ourselves. Notice the kinds of words you use to describe yourself and the thoughts you think about yourself."

Say, "Today we're going to *elevate* our confidence. Let's look at some words you've probably heard before. Let's really think about these words in a new way." Introduce each word and guide the discussion using the questions below.

GREAT

- ➡ Have you heard of the word *great*?

- ➡ Where did you hear the word *great*?

- ➡ Who can put the word *great* in a sentence?

- ➡ What do you think the word *great* means?

- ➡ What does it mean to be *great*?

- ➡ What types of things are going on in your life when you feel *great*?

SUCCEED

- ➡ Have you heard of the word *succeed*?

- ➡ Where did you hear the word *succeed*?

- ➡ Who said it to you?

- ➡ Who can put *succeed* in a sentence?

- ➡ What do you think the word *succeed* means?

- ➡ What does it mean to succeed?

- ➡ Tell me about a time when you succeeded.

CONFIDENCE

- ➡ Have you heard of the word *confidence*?

- ➡ Where did you hear the word *confidence*?

➡ Who said it to you?

➡ Who can put *confidence* in a sentence?

➡ What do you think the word *confidence* means?

➡ *Confidence* means "I know who I am" and that how *you* feel about yourself is most important. *You* have the power to *believe* you are *great*, no matter what anyone else may think.

UNIQUE

➡ Have you heard of the word *unique*?

➡ How would you feel if someone told you that you are unique?

➡ What do you think the word *unique* means?

➡ What does it mean for a person to be unique?

➡ What is unique about you?

➡ Does anyone else's laugh sound just like yours?

➡ Does anyone else's handwriting look just like yours?

➡ What else is uniquely you? Your voice? Maybe you have dance moves that are all your own, or you are really good at spelling difficult words.

ELEVATE

➡ Have you heard of the word *elevate*?

➡ When you practice something new, do you get better at it? Practicing *elevated* your abilities!

➡ Has anyone ever made you feel elevated?

➡ Have you ever made anyone feel elevated?

➡ What does it mean to elevate, and why do you think we named this program ELEVATE!?

Say, "We named this program ELEVATE! because we believe there is greatness and success in every child and adult who participates. That's why we call ourselves ELEVATE! superstars! Every one of us is a superstar. We elevate how we act and how we learn so that we can shine brighter and brighter and rise higher and higher. Now we're going to do a short activity so each of us can see how we think about ourselves. We want you to find *your* unique areas of greatness and think about the people who bring greatness out in you. I'm going to read a few sentences, and I want you to fill in the blank at the end of each sentence."

You may have the children raise their hands to share or call out their answers popcorn-style. Give appropriate instructions and encourage full participation by all students using the question prompt after you read the sentence with the blank if you don't get any responses or after a lull. Allow several students to share with each sentence. Thank them for their willingness to share with the group and affirm each child.

➡ I am great because _____

_____

_____.

➡ I admire _____
because _____

_____

_____.

➡ The great things that I expect to happen for me include

_____

_____

_____
_____.

→ I am good at _____
_____
_____
_____.

→ My friends are good at _____
_____
_____.

→ When I need help, I go to _____
_____
_____.

→ Some important people who look like me are _____
_____
_____.

→ I like to do _____
_____
_____with my free time.

ELEVATE! READING CIRCLE

The ELEVATE! curriculum features easy-to-read illustrated books about children from different backgrounds. Each of the recommended books is available online. Place children in age-appropriate small groups. Read the story, then explore the discussion questions, which help measure reading comprehension, enhance understanding of key themes, and engage students with the story and its connection to the theme.

BOOK SELECTION: *I Like Myself!*

If you have enough staff members or volunteers, move the children into small groups for reading time with one adult per group. Hold up the cover of the book *I Like Myself!* by Karen Beaumont and David Catrow.

Ask, "What do you think this story might be about?" Invite responses. Remain curious and ask students to elaborate on their thoughts. Read the selected book.

We Grow Together

DISCUSSION QUESTIONS: *I Like Myself!*

➡ How was the main character unique?

➡ Would you be the main character's friend? Do you think everyone would want to be the main character's friend? Why or why not?

➡ What might some children tease our main character about?

➡ How do you think the main character would respond to teasing?

➡ How should we treat people who are unique or different?

➡ How should we respond when other people point out things about us that are unique or different?

We Strive Together

Lesson plans will include ELEVATE! Wise Words. The Wise Words vocabulary will be connected to the reading lesson designed to build language skills and help students meet Common Core benchmarks. Below, the focus is broken down by grade level.

Kindergartners: The goal we are striving for is letter recognition. Encourage the students to identify all the words in the story that begin with a certain letter and talk about what the word means. This can be done for multiple letters per story. Some students may be ready to advance to matching letters with sounds and identifying syllables in multisyllable words.[1]

First Graders: The goal to strive for is segmenting and blending phonemes, which are *perceptually distinct units of sound in a specified language that distinguish one word from another*, in other words segmenting parts of the word out and blending them together to read one-syllable words. For example, "nose"—*n, o, s,* silent *e* = nose. Some students may be ready to move on to isolating and pronouncing vowel sounds along with phonemes in spoken single-syllable words.[2]

Second Graders: The goal is phonics and word recognition, beginning with identifying vowel sounds within words. Some students may be able to decode regularly spelled two-syllable words with long vowels.[3]

Third Graders: The goal is to identify prefixes and suffixes and decode multisyllable words. Third graders should be encouraged to read accurately and with increased fluency, applying phonics skills to sound out unfamiliar words and utilizing context clues to determine the meaning of those words.[4]

---

1   Common Core State Standards Initiative, "English Language Arts Standards," accessed September 3, 2021, http://www.corestandards.org/ELA-Literacy/RF/K/1/d/.

2   Ibid., accessed September 3, 2021, http://www.corestandards.org/ELA-Literacy/RF/1/2/b/ and http://www.corestandards.org/ELA-Literacy/RF/1/2/c/.

3   Ibid., accessed September 3, 2021, http://www.corestandards.org/ELA-Literacy/RF/2/3/b/ and http://www.corestandards.org/ELA-Literacy/RF/2/3/b/.

4   Ibid., accessed September 3, 2021, http://www.corestandards.org/ELA-Literacy/RF/3/3/a/ and http://www.corestandards.org/ELA-Literacy/RF/3/3/c/.

WISE WORDS

General Vocabulary

➡ Great

➡ Succeed

➡ Unique

➡ Confidence

I Like Myself! *Vocabulary*

Grades K–1		**Grades 2–3**
Me	Different	Inside
Like	Wild	Around
Eyes	Tame	Everywhere
Ears	Fast	
Nose	Slow	
Same	Think	

We Work Together

ELEVATE! ARTS AND CRAFTS

Each lesson will include an arts and crafts project that aligns with the theme of the unit. This will allow students to expand the lesson further and apply and expand upon the new learning through other types of intelligence and experiences. To explore the topic of elevating confidence with a focus on each child choosing to develop confidence through the lesson theme, engage the children in making a personalized ELEVATE! tote bag.

Gather supplies listed below in advance. If you are teaching virtually, adapt instructions and provide an arts and crafts kit that the parents or caregivers may pick up or that you send home for children. For this activity, consider the cultural composition of your classroom. Look at the demographic information and include symbols that represent the various cultures of students in your class.

MATERIALS

- cloth tote bag
- poster board
- 3"–4" letter stencils
- fabric
- fabric glue
- scissors
- gemstones
- feathers
- stickers
- other decorative items and cultural symbols

INSTRUCTIONS

1. Using an alphabet stencil, students should trace and cut out their first and last initials. If the stencils are a size that will allow the full first name to fit across the bag, then the child can put their first name on the front of the bag.

2. Have the children glue stencil cutouts of their name or initials to the front of their tote bags. Students can then glue other decora-

tive items, such as gemstones, feathers, and stickers, onto their bags as well. They can also use fabric to make shapes and glue these onto the surface of their ELEVATE! tote bag.

3. Students can use this bag to carry items to and from ELEVATE! and for special art projects. Share ideas with the children about how they might use their bag as they are completing this activity. Invite them to share their ideas for how they might use their personalized tote bag.

4. Remind students that each of them is one of a kind. Suggest to the children that they take a look around the room and notice the variety of children and adults and all the unique tote bags created.

5. If you'd like, gather for a class photo to decorate your classroom walls. Note that you should not share this photograph publicly unless you have obtained permission from all parents of the children participating in your ELEVATE! after-school program.

6. Clean up from the arts and crafts experience and gather the children for closing thoughts and the "ELEVATE! Superstars" song.

We Rise Together

Pause to review the progress for the day or for the week. Reinforce this lesson's key themes with your students, affirming their progress and participation.

"ELEVATE! SUPERSTARS"

→ [Child's name/group name/class name] is a superstar!

→ [Child's achievement] makes [her/him] a superstar!

→ Keep shooting for the stars, ELEVATE! superstars!

→ We love to watch you elevate!

ELEVATING OUR CIRCLE

ELEVATE! Focus:
Elevating Our Circle

We are stronger together. When we work together with classmates, members of our family, and members of our community, we can achieve great things.

ELEVATE! Objective:
Demonstrate Working Together

Students will work together with their classmates to readily recognize and articulate the value of elevating our circle. Over time, students will more readily move toward cooperation and shared activities and make choices that elevate friends and family, their own unique values, and everyone around them.

ELEVATE! Reading: Books for Elevating Our Circle

→ *Florence and Her Fantastic Family Tree* by Judy Gilliam and Laura Addari

→ *Skin Like Mine* by LaTashia M. Perry

→ *Our Class Is a Family* by Shannon Olsen and Sandie Sonke

→ *Have You Filled a Bucket Today?* by Carol McCloud and David Messing

ELEVATE! Family Support: Elevating Our Circle

Support the child's experience during this unit of ELEVATE! through encouraging and affirming conversations around the ELEVATE! focus and learning objective above. Find opportunities to point out positive choices your child makes to elevate their circle and to include friends and family members, classmates, and people they encounter every day.

LESSON 1: ELEVATING FAMILY

We Shine Together

Say, "Welcome, everyone! Are we ready to *elevate*?" Encourage the children to respond actively and with enthusiasm.

Ask the three daily questions in the ELEVATE! Affirmations section below. You may wish to call on children or simply post the question to the whole group and wait for responses. Invite the children to use their imagination to try new ways to elevate their day and the experience of their classmates.

ELEVATE! AFFIRMATIONS

"Today I feel _____

_____

_____."

"I can make my day better by _____

_____

_____."

"I can help make _____'s day
better by _____

_____

_____."

Remind the children that it's OK to begin where they are. Say, "No matter what kind of day you're having, who you are and how you are is just fine because, together, we can ..." Wait for the children to respond with "*Elevate!*"

Say, "That's right! Together, we can elevate! Today we'll be talking about how we can elevate our *family*. But first, let's do our ELEVATE! Affirmations. I'm going to read each affirmation, and I want to invite *you* to raise your hand if you'd like to share an affirmation today."

Allow three or four responses per question. If time allows, give students time for further reflection and expression, wherever possible focusing on a positive trajectory for their day from here. Ensure that all children are given the opportunity to participate over the course of your after-school program.

"ELEVATE! AFFIRMATION" SONG

Beginning each lesson with the affirmation song allows you, the teacher, to set the cultural tone for the classroom—a tone that tells the students that everyone is welcome and that each and every child will be loved and accepted for their unique traits and abilities. Students can sing along with the recorded version.

Encourage all students to express themselves by singing or participating in a way that feels good to them. You might make instruments available, for example, and encourage the children to clap or snap their fingers to keep the rhythm. If you choose, you may also encourage body movements, such as swaying from side to side, dancing creatively, or jumping on the word *elevate*.

Mathematicians and artists,

Musicians and lyricists,

They are all gifts;

They are loved at ELEVATE!

Athletes and readers,

Supporters and leaders,

All kinds of believers

Are loved at ELEVATE!

Hair kinky or straight,

Long tresses or a fade,

Eyes of all shapes

Are loved at ELEVATE!

Fair skin

To every shade of melanin,

We are all kin;

You are loved at ELEVATE!

A temperament that's mild

Or with a little bit of spice,

Personas of all types

Are loved at ELEVATE!

At ELEVATE!

Everybody can find their place;

Never have to worry about feeling hate.

Everybody's loved at ELEVATE!

We Learn Together

ELEVATE! FOCUS

Introduce the theme of this unit, elevating our circle. The ELEVATE! focus for students is elevating family. Guide the children in a discussion of these themes using the suggested conversation highlights below.

Say, "Today we're going to *elevate* our lives and the lives of the people around us by elevating how we think about family. Let's look at some words you've probably heard before. Let's really think about these words in a new way." Introduce each word and guide the discussion using the questions below.

HARMONY

➡ Have you heard of the word *harmony*?

➡ Where have you heard the word *harmony*?

➡ Who can put the word *harmony* in a sentence?

➡ What do you think *harmony* means?

➡ What does it mean to have harmony?

➡ When have you felt harmony?

FAMILY

➡ Have you ever heard of the word *family*?

➡ Where have you heard the word *family*?

➡ Who can put the word *family* in a sentence?

➡ What does *family* mean to you?

➡ Who is in your family?

➡ Is family only the people you live with?

➡ Do you feel harmony with your family?

Say, "Now we're going to do a short activity about our theme of *family*."

For grades K–1, use a chalk or smart board to list out all of the letters of the word *family*, placing each letter on a separate line: F-A-M-I-L-Y. Leave a space after each letter to add a phrase or sentence that begins with the letters you have listed.

For grades 2 and up, you can give each child a sheet of paper and ask them to put each letter that spells *family* on each line.

Say, "We're going to think of words or short phrases that begin with these letters that describe how you feel about your family. Let's start with *F*. Who has a word or phrase?" Allow time for responses.

If students need more guidance, you might ask, "What's a word to describe your experience of family? Fun? Fantastic? Forgiving?"

Note: This activity can also be done as a group. For a group activity, print out pictures or words that represent family, based on the letters making up the word *family*. For example, you might find a picture of a birthday party that could represent the word *fun* for the *F* in *family*. Students can then choose as a group which picture, word, or phrase matches each letter.

Use images of different types of families—interracial families, intergenerational families, families who don't seem to be related by blood. Ask, "Do any of these families remind you of your family?" Allow several children to share about which picture reminds them of their family and why.

When you have the first letters written on the chalkboard or smart board, say, "For each letter, please give me a word or a sentence that represents family for you, or tell me what *family* means to you.

Write one word, phrase, or sentence for each of the letters. As an example, for *F*, you might write 'friends' or 'fun playing games.' For *M*, you might write 'My mom makes great food.'"

Say, "Thank you, everyone! You just built what is called an *acrostic poem*. We build acrostic poems by using the first letter of each word to make the lines. Now everyone can share their acrostic poems. As we listen to these poems, let's think about these questions.

➡ What makes up a family?

➡ Does *family* have to mean we are related to someone directly?

➡ Does someone have to live in our house to be considered family?

➡ Is ELEVATE! a family? Why or why not?

➡ How do we treat our fellow family members?

➡ How *should* we treat our fellow family members?

➡ How *should* we treat our family members in ELEVATE!?

➡ Do you think harmony is important in a family? Why or why not?"

ELEVATE! READING CIRCLE

The ELEVATE! curriculum features easy-to-read illustrated books about children from different backgrounds. Each of the recommended books is available online. Place children in age-appropriate small groups. Read the story, then explore the discussion questions, which help measure reading comprehension, enhance understanding of key themes, and engage students with the story and its connection to the theme.

BOOK SELECTION:
Florence and Her Fantastic Family Tree

➡ If you have enough staff members or volunteers, move the children into small groups for reading time with one adult per group.

➡ Hold up the cover of the book *Florence and Her Fantastic Family Tree* by Judy Gilliam and Laura Addari. Ask, "What do you think this story might be about?" Invite responses. Remain curious and ask students to elaborate on their thoughts.

➡ Read the book.

We Grow Together

DISCUSSION QUESTIONS:
Florence and Her Fantastic Family Tree

➡ Who did Florence include in her family tree?

➡ Were they all blood relatives?

➡ Did her family tree grow larger or smaller over time?

➡ Do the family members welcome new people to the family tree?

➡ Do any of you know of a family like Florence's family?

➡ Do you think it's always easy for families to get along as they grow or as new people join the family?

➡ Do you think it's always easy for families to get along when they are not blood relatives?

➡ Why do you think Florence was worried about her family size?

➡ What would you say to Florence if you were in the story?

Say, "In the book *Florence*, we saw how her family grew. Her family grew even as one side of the family broke up. For those of us who come from families where parents may not live together, it can sometimes create new possibilities to make our families larger and receive more love. Just like Florence's extended family, you can look at your fellow ELEVATE! superstars and your teachers as a part of your family. If you count your ELEVATE! family members, then we *all* have a big, fantastic family tree!"

We Strive Together

Lesson plans will include ELEVATE! Wise Words. The Wise Words vocabulary will be connected to the reading lesson designed to build language skills and help students meet Common Core benchmarks. Below, the focus is broken down by grade level.

Kindergartners: The goal we are striving for is letter recognition. Encourage students to identify all the words in the story that start with a certain letter and then talk about what that word means. This can be done for multiple letters per story. Some students may be ready to advance to matching letters with sounds and identifying syllables in multisyllable words.[5]

First Graders: The goal to strive for is segmenting and blending phonemes, *perceptually distinct units of sound in a specified language that distinguish one word from another*, in other words segmenting parts of the word out and blending them together to read one syllable words. For example, "nose"—*n*, *o*, *s*, silent *e* = nose. Some students may be ready to move on to isolating and pronouncing vowel sounds along with phonemes in spoken single-syllable words.[6]

---

5   Common Core State Standards Initiative, "English Language Arts Standards," accessed September 3, 2021, http://www.corestandards.org/ELA-Literacy/RF/K/1/d/.

6   Ibid., accessed September 3, 2021, http://www.corestandards.org/ELA-Literacy/RF/1/2/b/ and http://www.corestandards.org/ELA-Literacy/RF/1/2/c/.

Second Graders: The goal is phonics and word recognition, beginning with identifying vowel sounds within words. Some students may be able to decode regularly spelled two-syllable words with long vowels.[7]

Third Graders: The goal is to identify prefixes and suffixes and decode multisyllable words. Third graders should be encouraged to read accurately and with increased fluency, applying phonics skills to sound out unfamiliar words and utilizing context clues to determine the meaning of those words.[8]

WISE WORDS

General Vocabulary

➡ Family

➡ Acrostic

➡ Harmony

Florence and Her Fantastic Family Tree *Vocabulary*

Grades K–1		**Grades 2–3**
Tree	Giant	Counting
Six	Kids	Parents
Wife	Worry	Original
Space	Trunk	Classroom
Wall	Loud	Family
Son	Crazy	Stepmother
		Half brother
		Confused
		Describe

---

7   Ibid., accessed September 3, 2021, http://www.corestandards.org/ELA-Literacy/RF/2/3/b/ and http://www.corestandards.org/ELA-Literacy/RF/2/3/b/.

8   Ibid., accessed September 3, 2021, http://www.corestandards.org/ELA-Literacy/RF/3/3/a/ and http://www.corestandards.org/ELA-Literacy/RF/3/3/c/.

We Work Together

ELEVATE! ARTS AND CRAFTS

Each lesson will include arts and crafts projects specific to the unit. This will allow students to expand the lesson further by applying it to other types of intelligence and experiences. To explore the topic of elevating our circle with a focus on elevating family, engage the children in a crafting activity to make a family tree pillowcase.

MATERIALS

- → pillowcase
- → fabric paint or permanent marker
- → glue
- → stones in the color of birthstones (use an assortment of stones matching birthstone colors)

INSTRUCTIONS

1. Each child should use fabric paint or a permanent marker to draw a tree that fills the majority of the front of the pillowcase. Have the children create branches for each family member they want to include on their tree.

2. Have students look up the birthstone for each family member. If a student does not know a family member's birth month, have that student choose a color that reminds them of that particular family member.

3. Invite the child to glue the selected stones on their branches.

4. When the family tree is complete, have the children paint or write their family name on the pillowcase. Assist younger children as needed.

5. Other craft items, such as feathers, beads, and sticky letters, may also be used to decorate each child's family tree pillowcase.

6. Clean up from the arts and crafts experience and gather the children for closing thoughts and the "ELEVATE! Superstars" song.

GROUP ACTIVITY

Allow each child to show his or her pillowcase. Ask the children to share which names they placed on their family tree and why they included this person.

CLOSING REFLECTION

Pause to review the progress for the day or the week. Reinforce this lesson's key themes with the students, affirming their progress and participation.

Say, "In today's lesson, we talked about family and who can be a part of our family. We also talked about different types of families, and we were reminded that members of our family don't have to be blood relatives. We also talked about how to treat members of our family.

"You can use the pillowcase you made today to remind you of the people who are important to you and to remind you to treat them like they are special. We want to be thankful for the time we get to spend with members of our family—our families in our homes and our ELEVATE! family. Your family tree pillowcase can remind us to be grateful for the memories we create with our families."

We Rise Together

Pause to review the progress for the day or the week. Reinforce this lesson's key themes with your students, affirming their progress and participation.

"ELEVATE! SUPERSTARS"

➡ [Child's name/group name/class name] is a superstar!

➡ [Child's achievement] makes [her/him] a superstar!

➡ Keep shooting for the stars, ELEVATE! superstars!

➡ We love to watch you elevate!

ELEVATING COOPERATION

ELEVATE! Focus: Elevating Cooperation

We can work together. Teamwork and cooperation create a space for everyone to rise. When we come together and cooperate, we elevate ourselves and others.

ELEVATE! Objective: Demonstrate Cooperation

Students will recognize the value of cooperating with others—in the classroom, at home, and in their everyday lives. They will see the connection between adopting a spirit of cooperation and positive life outcomes. Over time, students will become more and more cooperative, contributing fully and allowing space for others to contribute. They will increasingly make choices and take positive actions that demonstrate a spirit of cooperation.

ELEVATE! Reading: Books for Elevating Cooperation

→ *Teamwork Isn't My Thing, and I Don't Like to Share!* by Julia Cook and Kelsey De Weerd

→ *Bring Me Some Apples and I'll Make You a Pie* by Robbin Gourley

→ *Those Shoes* by Maribeth Boelts

→ *All Are Welcome* by Alexandra Penfold and Suzanne Kaufman

ELEVATE! Family Support: Elevating Cooperation

Support your child's experience during this unit of ELEVATE! through encouraging and affirming conversations that focus on ways to work together. Notice your child's level of cooperation. Speak words of positive affirmation and belief to your student. Encourage your child to share more of who they are and to enter into new social situations with a spirit of cooperation.

Students will become more and more cooperative, contributing fully and allowing space for others to contribute.

LESSON 2: ELEVATING COORDINATION

We Shine Together

Say, "Welcome, everyone! Are we ready to *elevate*?" Encourage the children to respond actively and with enthusiasm.

Ask the three daily questions in the ELEVATE! Affirmations section below. You may wish to call on children or simply post the question to the whole group and wait for responses. Invite the children to use their imagination to try new ways to elevate their day and the experience of their classmates.

ELEVATE! AFFIRMATIONS

"Today I feel _____
_____
_____."

"I can make my day better by _____
_____
_____."

"I can help make _____'s day
better by _____
_____
_____."

Remind the children that it's OK to begin where they are. Say, "No matter what kind of day you're having, who you are and how you are is just fine because, together, we can ..." Wait for the children to respond with "*Elevate!*"

Say, "That's right! Together, we can elevate! Today we'll be talking about how we can elevate *coordination*. But first, let's do our ELEVATE! affirmations. I'm going to read each affirmation, and I want to invite *you* to raise your hand if you'd like to share an affirmation today."

Allow three or four responses per question. If time allows, give students time for further reflection and expression, wherever possible focusing on a positive trajectory for their day from here. Ensure that all children are given the opportunity to participate over the course of your after-school program.

"ELEVATE! AFFIRMATION" SONG

Beginning each lesson with the affirmation song allows you, the teacher, to set the cultural tone for the classroom—a tone that tells the students that everyone is welcome and that each and every child will be loved and accepted for their unique traits and abilities. Students can sing along with the recorded version.

Encourage all students to express themselves by singing or participating in a way that feels good to them. You might make instruments available, for example, and encourage children to clap or snap their fingers to keep the rhythm. If you choose, you may also encourage body movements, such as swaying from side to side, dancing creatively, or jumping on the word *elevate*.

Mathematicians and artists,

Musicians and lyricists,

They are all gifts;

They are loved at ELEVATE!

Athletes and readers,

Supporters and leaders,

All kinds of believers

Are loved at ELEVATE!

Hair kinky or straight,

Long tresses or a fade,

Eyes of all shapes

Are loved at ELEVATE!

Fair skin

To every shade of melanin,

We are all kin;

You are loved at ELEVATE!

A temperament that's mild

Or with a little bit of spice,

Personas of all types

Are loved at ELEVATE!

At ELEVATE!

Everybody can find their place;

Never have to worry about feeling hate.

Everybody's loved at ELEVATE!

We Learn Together

ELEVATE! FOCUS

Introduce the theme of this unit—elevating cooperation. The ELEVATE! focus in this lesson is elevating coordination. Guide the children in a discussion of these themes using the suggested conversation highlights below.

Say, "Today we're going to *elevate* our *cooperation* by elevating *coordination*. Let's look at some words you've probably heard before in a new way." Introduce each word and guide the discussion using the questions below.

COORDINATION

- ➡ Have you ever heard of the word *coordination*?
- ➡ Where have you heard this word *coordination*?
- ➡ What do you think *coordination* means?

INSTRUCTIONS

- ➡ Have you ever heard of the word *instructions*?
- ➡ Where have you heard this word *instructions*?
- ➡ What do you think *instructions* means?

TIMING

- ➡ Have you ever heard of the word *timing*?
- ➡ Where have you heard the word *timing*?
- ➡ What do you think *timing* means?

RESTAURANT

➡ Have you ever heard of the word *restaurant*?

➡ Where have you heard the word *restaurant*?

➡ What do you think *restaurant* means?

➡ How many of you like to eat at restaurants?

➡ What are some restaurants that you like?

Say, "Do you think coordination, instructions, and timing are important qualities to have when you are working in a restaurant? Why or why not?" Allow for several minutes of discussion.

Before class, print off pictures of opening the doors, cleaning up the kitchen, cutting the vegetables, frying the hamburger and fries, using the cash register, and delivering or serving food to customers. Spread the pictures out or project them on a screen so students can see them.

Use this opportunity to ask students about their favorite restaurants or favorite places to eat other than home. Ask them their favorite foods to eat at those places. This gives students an opportunity to share the foods they like to eat, which may represent different cultural backgrounds and preferences.

Say, "Now we're going to do a short activity about the importance of coordination, instructions, and timing in a restaurant environment. ELEVATE! superstars, we need to put these in order so that the customer can get their hamburgers."

Ask, "Should the person who is handling the cash register be the person who slices the vegetables?" Wait for responses.

"Should the same person who is frying the hamburgers also fry the french fries? Why or why not?" Wait for responses, then say, "In a restaurant, each team member has a specific role. If the person preparing the food also had to collect the customer's money and give them change, the restaurant team would not likely be able to coordinate their activities and deliver the customer's food on time."

Ask, "Can we cook the food before the doors are opened?" Wait for responses, then ask, "How about this: can the cooks clean up at the same time they are cooking the food? Why or why not?"

Ask, "What happens if the kitchen is not cleaned after food is cooked?" Wait for responses, then ask, "What happens if the kitchen is not cleaned at the end of the day?"

"In a restaurant, there is an order of things that need to happen. Timing is important. Following instructions and working together as a team is important. When each team member coordinates his or her activity with the activities of other members of the team, the customer has a better experience. Today we're going to read a story that talks about elevating coordination. Let's gather for our reading circle."

ELEVATE! READING CIRCLE

The ELEVATE! curriculum features easy-to-read illustrated books about children from different backgrounds. Each of the recommended books is available online. Place children in age-appropriate small groups. Read the story, then explore the discussion questions, which help measure reading comprehension, enhance understanding of key themes, and engage students with the story and its connection to the theme.

BOOK SELECTION:
Bring Me Some Apples and I'll Make You a Pie

➡ If you have enough staff members or volunteers, move the children into small groups for reading time with one adult per group.

➡ Hold up the cover of the book *Bring Me Some Apples and I'll Make You a Pie* by Robbin Gourley. Ask, "What do you think this story might be about?" Invite responses. Remain curious and ask students to elaborate on their thoughts.

➡ Read the selected book.

We Grow Together

DISCUSSION QUESTIONS:
Bring Me Some Apples and I'll Make You a Pie

➡ Where do you think this story took place? How long ago do you think this story took place?

➡ Who did Edna work with to collect honey?

➡ What kinds of fruits did Edna collect?

➡ Did Edna harvest the fruits and peaches alone? Who was with her?

➡ How do you think Edna and her family got all of this work accomplished? Did you hear anything in the story about them arguing? What did they do instead?

➡ What do you think might have happened if Edna and her family had not worked together in cooperation and coordinated their activities?

➡ How did each person in the story make a contribution?

➡ How do you think learning to cooperate helped Edna become a famous chef?

Say, "In the book *Bring Me Some Apples and I'll Make You a Pie* by Robbin Gourley, we saw that when you cooperate, you can gain more. Edna's family had more food to eat because they had more people to help harvest the food.

"Had only Edna's parents or grandma harvested the food, they would have had far less. They may not have had enough for everyone to eat, period. Remember, in the wintertime, they couldn't harvest. So not only did they have to work together to harvest plenty of food but everyone also had to follow instructions on how to pick the food, clean the food, and store the food! Had they not picked, cleaned, and stored the food correctly, it would have spoiled by the wintertime. I'm sure that these skills helped Edna become a famous chef.

"In a restaurant, it takes several people to create enough food to serve the public. Each person has to do their part and follow instructions, or the food could be burned, it could get cold, it could be dropped. Or if people really aren't paying attention to their jobs, the restaurant could even catch on fire. Working together by coordinating our activities makes everything possible. When we coordinate, we elevate! When we cooperate, we elevate!"

We Strive Together

Lesson plans will include ELEVATE! Wise Words. The Wise Words vocabulary will be connected to the reading lesson designed to build language skills and help students meet Common Core benchmarks. Below, the focus is broken down by grade level.

Kindergartners: The goal we are striving for is recognition of common high-frequency words by sight (e.g., *the, of, to, you, she, my, is, are, do, does*). Encourage students to identify these words and read them aloud.[9]

---

9   Common Core State Standards Initiative, "English Language Arts Standards," accessed September 3, 2021, http://www.corestandards.org/ELA-Literacy/RF/K/3/c/.

First Graders: The goal to strive for is using knowledge that every syllable must have a vowel sound to determine the number of syllables in a printed word and decoding two-syllable words following basic patterns by breaking the words into syllables.[10]

Second Graders: The goal is to master spelling-sound correspondences for additional common vowel teams and decode regularly spelled two-syllable words with long vowels.[11]

Third Graders: The goal is to utilize context to confirm or self-correct word recognition and understanding, rereading as necessary.[12]

WISE WORDS

General Vocabulary

➡ Coordination

➡ Instructions

➡ Timing

➡ Restaurant

➡ Cooperation

---

10   Ibid., accessed September 3, 2021, http://www.corestandards.org/ELA-Literacy/RF/1/3/d/ and http://www.corestandards.org/ELA-Literacy/RF/1/3/e/.

11   Ibid., accessed September 3, 2021, http://www.corestandards.org/ELA-Literacy/RF/2/3/b/ and http://www.corestandards.org/ELA-Literacy/RF/2/3/c/.

12   Ibid., accessed September 3, 2021, http://www.corestandards.org/ELA-Literacy/RF/3/4/c/.

Bring Me Some Apples and I'll Make You a Pie *Vocabulary*

Grades K–1	**Grades 2–3**
Chef	Famous
Edna	Collecting
Greens	Delicious
Roots	Lettuce
Tea	Wintertime
Ails	Questions
Bread	Walnut
	Saved
	Gathering

We Work Together

ELEVATE! ARTS AND CRAFTS

Each lesson will include arts and crafts projects specific to the unit. This will allow students to expand the lesson further by applying it to other types of intelligence and experiences. To explore the topic of elevating cooperation and elevating coordination, engage the children in making an ELEVATE! cooperation chart.

MATERIALS

➡ a large ELEVATE! logo printed and laminated for posting on the wall

➡ stenciled letters spelling "cooperation chart"

➡ classroom jobs written or printed on small, vertical, standing envelopes

➡ stars stenciled on poster board (one poster for each child)

➡ wooden sticks

➡ stick-on decorations, such as stars and jewels (be mindful of weight)

➡ glue

➡ scissors

➡ tape

INSTRUCTIONS

1. Prepare enough envelopes for each child to have a classroom job. Examples of classroom jobs include sharpening pencils, passing out supplies, serving as the line leader or the line caboose, helping take attendance, or cleaning up at the end of the day. You can also add in an affirmation song leader or a "bucket filler" as we talked about in unit 2. You can also assign students to help clean or pass out supplies for various activities to ensure all students have an opportunity to participate.

2. Each child should cut out their star, put their name on the star, and decorate their star with the materials provided.

3. Collaborative group activity: Based upon behavior and coop-eration, call each student up one by one to select a job on the chart. As they choose a job, ask them how that job helps the ELEVATE! Express run better. If a child's first choice has already been taken, explain to the student how his or her contribu-tion helps the ELEVATE! Express. Involve the other students in providing affirmations for why this student's contribution is vital to the group. To encourage students to participate fully, say, "If we don't carry out all of the tasks, then we can't move on to the things we like to do."

4. Clean up from the arts and crafts experience and gather children for closing thoughts and the "ELEVATE! Superstars" song.

CLOSING REFLECTION

Pause to review the progress for the day or the week. Reinforce this lesson's key themes with the students, affirming their progress and participation.

Say, "In today's lesson, we talked about coordination. When we cooperate and coordinate our activities, it's important to get along and appreciate one another. But we must also use our listening skills to make sure we're following instructions and completing tasks together. We must be sure we are applying our energy correctly and working together as a team.

"It is also important to do tasks in the right order. We can't operate as a unified circle until we have affirmed everyone. We can't learn until we come together in good spirits. We can't do the fun group activities and have recreation until we learn. When we are unified, cooperating and learning together, then we win. We do better in school. We are happier in ELEVATE! And our parents and teachers are happier with us."

We Rise Together

"ELEVATE! SUPERSTARS"

➡ [Child's name/group name/class name] is a superstar!

➡ [Child's achievement] makes [her/him] a superstar!

➡ Keep shooting for the stars, ELEVATE! superstars!

➡ We love to watch you elevate!

ELEVATING COMMUNITY

ELEVATE! Focus: Elevating Community

When we work together, we can achieve great things. When we come together in community, we elevate everyone.

ELEVATE! Objective: Demonstrate Community

Students will recognize the ways we are connected to one another. Over time, students will consistently take aligned action to work together with their peers in a collaborative manner. They will increasingly make choices and take positive actions to support and uplift their classmates and consider the impact of their actions on the larger community.

ELEVATE! Reading: Books for Elevating Community

→ *I Promise* by LeBron James and Nina Mata

→ *We Live Here Too!* by Nancy Loewen and Omarr Wesley

→ *Say Something!* by Peter Reynolds

→ *Grace Goes to Washington* by Kelly DiPucchio and LeUyen Pham

ELEVATE! Family Support: Elevating Community

Support the child's experience during this unit of ELEVATE! through encouraging and affirming conversations that focus on community.

Students will consistently take aligned action to work together with their peers in a collaborative manner.

Notice each child's level of understanding of and connection to the larger communities with which they are connected, from the classroom to the neighborhood. Speak words of positive affirmation and belief to your students and encourage them to believe in themselves as contributors to the larger community.

LESSON 2: ELEVATING CITIZENSHIP

We Shine Together

Say, "Welcome, everyone! Are we ready to *elevate*?" Encourage the children to respond actively and with enthusiasm.

Ask the three daily questions in the ELEVATE! Affirmations section below. You may wish to call on children or simply post the question to the whole group and wait for responses. Invite the children to use their imagination to try new ways to elevate their day and the experience of their classmates.

ELEVATE! AFFIRMATIONS

"Today I feel _____

_____

_____."

"I can make my day better by _____

_____

_____."

"I can help make _____'s day

better by _____

_____

_____."

Remind the children that it's OK to begin where they are. Say, "No matter what kind of day you're having, who you are and how you are is just fine because, together, we can …" Wait for children to respond with "*Elevate!*"

Say, "That's right! Together, we can elevate! Today we'll be talking about how we can elevate *citizenship*. But first, let's do our ELEVATE! affirmations. I'm going to read each affirmation, and I want to invite *you* to raise your hand if you'd like to share an affirmation today."

Allow three or four responses per question. If time allows, give students time for further reflection and expression, wherever possible focusing on a positive trajectory for their day from here. Ensure that all children are given the opportunity to participate over the course of your after-school program.

"ELEVATE! AFFIRMATION" SONG

Beginning each lesson with the affirmation song allows you, the teacher, to set the cultural tone for the classroom—a tone that tells the students that everyone is welcome and that each and every child will be loved and accepted for their unique traits and abilities. Students can sing along with the recorded version.

Encourage all students to express themselves by singing or participating in a way that feels good to them. You might make instruments available, for example, and encourage children to clap or snap their fingers to keep the rhythm. If you choose, you may also encourage body movements, such as swaying from side to side, dancing creatively, or jumping on the word *elevate*.

Mathematicians and artists,

Musicians and lyricists,

They are all gifts;

They are loved at ELEVATE!

Athletes and readers,

Supporters and leaders,

All kinds of believers

Are loved at ELEVATE!

Hair kinky or straight,

Long tresses or a fade,

Eyes of all shapes

Are loved at ELEVATE!

Fair skin

To every shade of melanin,

We are all kin;

You are loved at ELEVATE!

A temperament that's mild

Or with a little bit of spice,

Personas of all types

Are loved at ELEVATE!

At ELEVATE!

Everybody can find their place;

Never have to worry about feeling hate.

Everybody's loved at ELEVATE!

We Learn Together

ELEVATE! FOCUS

Introduce the theme of this unit—elevating community. The ELEVATE! focus in this lesson is elevating citizenship. Guide the children in a discussion of these themes using the suggested conversation highlights below.

Say, "Today we're going to *elevate* our *citizenship*. What do you think the word *citizenship* means?" Invite responses. "What do you think it means to be a good citizen?" Invite responses.

"Let's look at some words you've probably heard before and consider them in a new way." Introduce each word and guide the discussion using the questions below.

PARTICIPATE

- Have you ever heard of the word *participate*?

- What do you think *participate* means?

- Where have you heard the word *participate* before?

VOTE

- Have you ever heard of the word *vote*?

- What do you think *vote* means?

- Where have you heard the word *vote* before?

Ask each of the questions below, allowing time to discuss each one and provide guidance and examples:

- How do you think citizenship and voting may be related?

- How do you think citizenship and participation may be related?

➡ How do you think citizenship and service may be related?

➡ How do you think citizenship and cooperation may be related?

➡ How do you think citizenship and being a leader may be related?

Say, "Let's do a short activity. As a citizen of this country, of your city, and of ELEVATE!, you should have expectations. In this country, you can expect that laws protect you."

Ask, "What kinds of things can we expect as citizens of our city? For example, as a citizen, you can expect to go to school without paying unless you want to. Garbage is usually picked up once a week. There are buses for transportation, roads to drive on, and sidewalks to walk on. You can use libraries just because you are a citizen. They are free.

"When we become adults, we have the power to vote for people who we think will ensure that laws are in place to protect us. We vote for people who can run our schools, run our cities, run our states, and run our country to make sure that we have free education. We vote for people who take care of our streets and make laws to keep our streets safe. If those people do not take care of our cities, state, and country and if they do not put laws in place to keep us safe, we have the power to vote them out.

"In many schools, we can elect student leaders who talk to our teachers and principals about the things that matter to us. Today we're going to elect an ELEVATE! student leader who will report to your teachers the things you want to see in ELEVATE!

"Before we move on, let's come up with a list of traits for your ELEVATE! student leader. What type of person should they be?"

Write a list of qualities on the board or screen. Discuss why each quality is desirable in a leader who will represent all students.

Say, "Our elected ELEVATE! student leader definitely should be a good citizen. What do you think it means to be a good citizen?" Discuss briefly, then say, "The book we're going to read today may give us some clues on what it means to be a good citizen."

ELEVATE! READING CIRCLE

The ELEVATE! curriculum features easy-to-read illustrated books about children from different backgrounds. Each of the recommended books is available online. Place children in age-appropriate small groups. Read the story, then explore the discussion questions, which help measure reading comprehension, enhance understanding of key themes, and engage students with the story and its connection to the theme.

BOOK SELECTION: *We Live Here Too!*

➡ If you have enough staff members or volunteers, move the children into small groups for reading time with one adult per group.

➡ Hold up the cover of the book *We Live Here Too!* by Nancy Loewen and Omarr Wesley. Ask, "What do you think this story might be about?" Invite responses. Remain curious and ask students to elaborate on their thoughts.

➡ Read the selected book.

We Grow Together

DISCUSSION QUESTIONS: *We Live Here Too!*

➡ What did Frank say we should do when we're asked to make friends with someone who everyone else thinks seems weird?

➡ What did Frank say we should do when we're working on a team, and we don't feel that we're good enough?

➡ What did Frank say about how we should keep our space?

➡ What advice did Frank give about being given food that we may not like?

➡ What advice did Frank give about children and voting?

➡ What does it mean to be patriotic? What other examples did Frank give of how we could be better citizens?

Say, "In the book *We Live Here Too!* by Nancy Loewen, we learned that we are all citizens, which means we all need to participate in our community. Frank gave us several clues to being good citizens. He said good citizens make friends with those who may be different from them and reminded us that all of us are different in some way to others. He said that we should take a chance when we don't feel we're good at something and that we should work to keep our space clean. This includes our learning space, our bedrooms at home, and the shared spaces in our communities.

"As he was talking about decluttering, Frank reminded us about the importance of giving. Good citizens make good leaders. And our community needs good leaders. I am sure there are many, many great leaders among our ELEVATE! superstars!"

We Strive Together

Lesson plans will include ELEVATE! Wise Words. The Wise Words vocabulary will be connected to the reading lesson designed to build language skills and help students meet Common Core benchmarks. At this point, we start building on vocabulary and linking it back to the story—in addition to reinforcing phonetic concepts introduced in previous units. Below, the focus is broken down by grade level.

Kindergartners: With prompting and support, compare and contrast the adventures and experiences of characters in familiar stories (in this case, we're comparing *I Promise* to ELEVATE!), name the author and illustrator of a story and define the role of each in telling the story, describe the relationship between illustrations and the text in which they appear (e.g., what person, place, thing, or idea in the text an illustration depicts), and identify the reasons an author gives to support points in a text.[13]

First Graders: The goal for first graders is to use the illustrations and details in a text to describe its key ideas, identify the reasons an author gives to support points in a text, and identify basic similarities and differences between two texts on the same topic (e.g., in illustrations, descriptions, or procedures). Additionally, encourage range of reading and level of text complexity with prompts and support for the student to read informational texts appropriately complex for grade 1 and encourage craft and structure knowledge through the identification of words and phrases in stories or poems that suggest feelings or appeal to the senses.[14]

Second Graders: The goal is to describe how characters in a story respond to major events and challenges and identify the main purpose of a text, including what the author wants to answer, explain, or describe so that by the end of the year they can read and comprehend literature, including stories and poetry, in the grades 2–3 text complexity band proficiently, with scaffolding as needed at the high end of the range.[15]

---

13   Common Core State Standards Initiative, "English Language Arts Standards," accessed September 3, 2021, http://www.corestandards.org/ELA-Literacy/RL/K/.

14   Ibid., accessed September 3, 2021, http://www.corestandards.org/ELA-Literacy/RL/1/.

15   Ibid., accessed September 3, 2021, http://www.corestandards.org/ELA-Literacy/RL/2/.

Third Graders: The goal is to read with sufficient accuracy and fluency to support comprehension, read grade-level text with purpose and understanding, distinguish their own point of view from that of the narrator or of the characters, and determine the meaning of words and phrases as they are used in a text, distinguishing literal from nonliteral language.[16]

WISE WORDS

General Vocabulary

➡ Citizenship

➡ Participation

➡ Vote

➡ Community

We Live Here Too! *Vocabulary*

Grades K–1	Grades 2–3	
Lunch	Answers	Million
Recess	Fidget	Billion
True	Paleontologist	Languages
Care	Planet	Countries

---

16   Ibid., accessed September 3, 2021, http://www.corestandards.org/ELA-Literacy/RL/3/.

We Work Together

ELEVATE! ARTS AND CRAFTS

Each lesson will include arts and crafts projects specific to the unit. This will allow students to expand the lesson further by applying it to other types of intelligence and experiences. To explore the topic of elevating community and elevating citizenship, engage the children in designing their own ELEVATE! campaign sign.

Gather the supplies listed below in advance. If you are teaching virtually, adapt the instructions and provide an arts and crafts kit that the parents or caregivers may pick up or that you send home for the children.

MATERIALS

- ➡ assorted poster board
- ➡ long wooden sticks
- ➡ alphabet stencils or stick-on letters for kindergarten and first graders
- ➡ markers and colored pencils
- ➡ scissors
- ➡ glue
- ➡ gemstones and other stick-on decorating items
- ➡ photos of each child, printed in advance
- ➡ paint
- ➡ a ballot box for voting
- ➡ index cards for casting votes

INSTRUCTIONS:

1. Each child should construct a sign that states, "Superstar [their name] for ELEVATE! Student Leader." For kindergarten and first graders, you can stencil in "for ELEVATE! Student Leader" and allow them to color those letters. Each child should write their name.

2. After adding the narrative, students should color or decorate their sign as they choose.

3. Add each student's picture to the sign to create a personalized touch.

4. Give each student an opportunity to share his or her sign if they want to be considered for a student leader position. Ask each candidate why they want to be considered and help them draw connections between their pitch and the criteria that the class will use to determine a good citizen.

5. For each student who would like to run for a student leadership position, write that student's name on the board and allow students to vote by hand (though I would recommend that the child they are voting on put their head down). For older students, allow them to write the child's name they want to select on their index card.

6. Have all students with index cards cast their ballots by placing their vote in the ballot box.

7. Share the results of the class election. Congratulate the winners and those who ran, noting how the participation of all contributes to the elevation of the community.

8. Clean up from the arts and crafts experience and gather the children for closing thoughts and the "ELEVATE! Superstars" song.

We Rise Together

Pause to review the progress for the day or the week. Reinforce this lesson's key themes with the students, affirming their progress and participation.

Say, "In today's lesson, we talked about the importance of elevating citizenship. You made great signs and presented great reasons for why you all should be elected as leaders. We may only be able to elect one ELEVATE! student leader per class, but *all* of you are leaders. You may be a leader with your younger siblings or cousins or a leader in your family or in your neighborhood. And most of the time, somebody is watching you and looking up to you without telling you. So remember, *everyone* in ELEVATE! is a superstar."

"ELEVATE! SUPERSTARS"

➡ [Child's name/group name/class name] is a superstar!

➡ [Child's achievement] makes [her/him] a superstar!

➡ Keep shooting for the stars, ELEVATE! superstars!

➡ We love to watch you elevate!

ELEVATING EXPRESSION

ELEVATE! Focus: Elevating Expression

You are creative. When you explore and use your creative gifts, you elevate yourself, your friends and family, and your community.

ELEVATE! Objective: Demonstrate Expression

Students will see themselves as naturally creative and understand the rich diversity of creative gifts. Over time, students will become more confident in claiming and confidently expressing their gifts.

ELEVATE! Reading: Books for Elevating Expression

- *Beyoncé: Shine Your Light* by Sarah Warren and Geneva Bowers

- *The Electric Slide and Kai* by Kelly J. Baptist and Darnell Johnson

- *Even Monsters Need Haircuts* by Matthew McElligott

- *Maybe Something Beautiful* by F. Isabel Campoy and Theresa Howell

ELEVATE! Family Support: Elevating Expression

Support the child's experience during this unit of ELEVATE! through encouraging and affirming conversations that focus on expression. Notice each child's level of expressiveness and willingness to try new things and be creative in a variety of ways. Speak words of positive affirmation, belief, and encouragement to your child.

Students will see themselves as naturally creative and understand the rich diversity of creative gifts.

LESSON 4: SHARING OUR EXPRESSIONS

We Shine Together

Say, "Welcome, everyone! Are we ready to *elevate*?" Encourage the children to respond actively and with enthusiasm.

Ask the three daily questions in the ELEVATE! Affirmations section below. You may wish to call on children or simply post the question to the whole group and wait for responses. Invite the children to use their imagination to try new ways to elevate their day and the experience of their classmates.

ELEVATE! AFFIRMATIONS

"Today I feel _____
_____
_____."

"I can make my day better by _____
_____
_____."

"I can help make _____'s day
better by _____
_____
_____."

Remind the children that it's OK to begin where they are. Say, "No matter what kind of day you're having, who you are and how you are is just fine because, together, we can ..." Wait for the children to respond with "Elevate!"

Say, "That's right! Together, we can elevate! Today we'll be talking about how we can elevate our *expression*. But first, let's do our ELEVATE! affirmations. I'm going to read each affirmation, and I want to invite *you* to raise your hand if you'd like to share an affirmation today."

Allow three or four responses per question. If time allows, give students time for further reflection and expression, wherever possible focusing on a positive trajectory for their day from here. Ensure that all children are given the opportunity to participate over the course of your after-school program.

"ELEVATE! AFFIRMATION" SONG

Beginning each lesson with the affirmation song allows you, the teacher, to set the cultural tone for the classroom—a tone that tells the students that everyone is welcome and that each and every child will be loved and accepted for their unique traits and abilities. Students can sing along with the recorded version.

Encourage all students to express themselves by singing or participating in a way that feels good to them. You might make instruments available, for example, and encourage children to clap or snap their fingers to keep the rhythm. If you choose, you may also encourage body movements, such as swaying from side to side, dancing creatively, or jumping on the word *elevate*.

Mathematicians and artists,

Musicians and lyricists,

They are all gifts;

They are loved at ELEVATE!

Athletes and readers,

Supporters and leaders,

All kinds of believers

Are loved at ELEVATE!

Hair kinky or straight

Long tresses or a fade,

Eyes of all shapes

Are loved at ELEVATE!

Fair skin

To every shade of melanin,

We are all kin;

You are loved at ELEVATE!

A temperament that's mild

Or with a little bit of spice,

Personas of all types

Are loved at ELEVATE!

At ELEVATE!

Everybody can find their place;

Never have to worry about feeling hate.

Everybody's loved at ELEVATE!

We Learn Together

ELEVATE! FOCUS

Introduce the theme of this unit—elevating expression. The ELEVATE! focus in this lesson is elevating my goals. Guide the children in a discussion of these themes using the suggested conversation highlights below.

Say, "Today we're going to share our expression. What do you think the word *canvas* means? Let's look at some other words you've probably heard before. Let's really think about these words in a new way." Introduce each word and guide the discussion using the questions below.

MURAL

➡ Have you ever heard of the word *mural*?

➡ Where have you heard the word *mural*?

➡ What does the word *mural* mean?

COLLABORATE

➡ Have you ever heard of the word *collaborate*?

➡ Where have you heard the word *collaborate*?

➡ What does the word *collaborate* mean?

BEAUTIFUL

➡ Have you ever heard of the word *beautiful*?

➡ Where have you heard the word *beautiful*?

➡ What does the word *beautiful* mean?

POSSIBLE

➡ Have you ever heard of the word *possible*?

➡ Where have you heard the word *possible*?

➡ What does the word *possible* mean?

Say, "Let's do a short activity where we think about what's possible and what can be beautiful. I am going to show you some images [on a smart screen or printed images on a black board]. For each image, I want you to tell me how it might be possible to make the item in this image beautiful."

➡ Show the first image of a piece of scrap fabric. Once students weigh in, show an image of a quilt.

➡ Show the first image of an abandoned building. Once students weigh in, show them an image of a building with beautiful murals on it.

➡ Show the first image of old magazines. Then show artwork made from recycled magazines.

➡ Show the first image of plastic bottles. Then show an image of art made from plastic bottles.

➡ Show the first image of scrap metal. Then show an image of art made from scrap metal.

Say, "Thank you for your responses. Now we're going to read a story about a young girl who saw possibilities in her community to make it more beautiful and how she worked together with others in her community as a team to make it happen."

ELEVATE! READING CIRCLE

The ELEVATE! curriculum features easy-to-read illustrated books about children from different backgrounds. Each of the recommended books is available online. Place children in age-appropriate small groups. Read the story, then explore the discussion questions, which help measure reading comprehension, enhance understanding of key themes, and engage students with the story and its connection to the theme.

BOOK SELECTION: *Maybe Something Beautiful*

- ➡ If you have enough staff members or volunteers, move the children into small groups for reading time with one adult per group.

- ➡ Hold up the cover of the book *Maybe Something Beautiful* by F. Isabel Campoy and Theresa Howell. Ask, "Does anyone recognize the lady on the cover? What do you know about her? What do you think the story is going to be about?" Invite responses. Remain curious and ask students to elaborate on their thoughts.

- ➡ Read the selected book.

We Grow Together

DISCUSSION QUESTIONS:
Maybe Something Beautiful

- ➡ In what ways did our main character, Mira, use creativity at home?

- ➡ What types of expressions did Mira share with people in her community?

- ➡ Why did Mira start placing her expressions up in her neighborhood? How did her neighborhood look?

➡ What often happens when neighborhoods are gray and don't seem well taken care of? How are those neighborhoods often treated?

➡ When Mira saw that her expression made her neighborhood just a little less gray, what did she do?

➡ What did the muralist see in the neighborhood?

➡ Did Mira start painting on buildings by herself or with permission?

➡ How did Mira turn her gray neighborhood into something beautiful?

Say, "In the book *Maybe Something Beautiful,* we saw that we can find something beautiful in things that some people don't find to be valuable at all. Seeing possibilities is a part of being creative. When we are creative, not only do we find creative ways to express ourselves but we also find ways to bring people together to make our communities better.

"In ELEVATE!, I challenge each of you to find ways to see more possibilities, even when we are facing challenges. Use that positivity and creativity to get your peers excited about making our learning center beautiful by improving the way our classroom looks and how we treat one another."

We Strive Together

Lesson plans will include ELEVATE Wise Words. The Wise Words vocabulary will be connected to the reading lesson designed to build language skills and help students meet Common Core benchmarks. At this point, in addition to reinforcing phonetic concepts introduced in previous units, we will begin building on vocabulary and linking it back to the story. Below, the focus is broken down by grade level.

Kindergartners: With prompting and support, ask and answer questions about key details in a text. Identify characters, settings, and major events in a story. Ask and answer questions about unknown words in a text.[17]

First Graders: Ask and answer questions about key details in a text. Describe characters, settings, and major events in a story using key details.[18]

Second Graders: Identify the main purpose of a text, including what the author wants to answer, explain, or describe. Describe how characters in a story respond to major events and challenges. By the end of the year, read and comprehend literature, including stories and poetry, in the grades 2–3 text complexity band proficiently, with scaffolding as needed at the high end of the range.[19]

Third Graders: Describe characters in a story (e.g., their traits, motivations, or feelings) and explain how their actions contribute to the sequence of events. Refer to parts of stories, dramas, and poems when writing or speaking about a text using terms such as *chapter*, *scene*, and *stanza*; describe how each successive part builds on earlier sections.[20]

---

17   Common Core State Standards Initiative, "English Language Arts Standards," accessed September 3, 2021, http://www.corestandards.org/ELA-Literacy/RL/K/1/ and http://www.corestandards.org/ELA-Literacy/RL/K/3/.

18   Ibid., accessed September 3, 2021, http://www.corestandards.org/ELA-Literacy/RL/1/1/ and http://www.corestandards.org/ELA-Literacy/RL/1/3/.

19   Ibid., accessed September 3, 2021, http://www.corestandards.org/ELA-Literacy/RI/2/6/ and http://www.corestandards.org/ELA-Literacy/RI/2/10/.

20   Ibid., accessed September 3, 2021, http://www.corestandards.org/ELA-Literacy/RL/3/3/ and http://www.corestandards.org/ELA-Literacy/RL/3/5/.

WISE WORDS

General Vocabulary

➡ Canvas

➡ Expression

➡ Creativity

➡ Mural

➡ Collaborate

➡ Beautiful

Maybe Something Beautiful *Vocabulary*

Grades K–1	Grades 2–3
Shop	Glowing
Flowers	Police officer
Heart	Shadows
Wall	Thoughtful
Sky	Beautiful
Artist	Muralist
Lit	Loudest
Trouble	Scurried
Clothes	Imagined
Color	Muralist
Joy	

We Work Together

ELEVATE! ARTS AND CRAFTS

Each lesson will include arts and crafts projects specific to the unit. This will allow students to expand the lesson further by applying it to other types of intelligence and experiences. To explore the topic of elevating expression and sharing our expression, engage the children in a crafting activity to design an ELEVATE! community quilt.

MATERIALS

→ squares of fabric in a variety of colors (for those students who represent cultures other than European, be sure to research and include fabrics that represent their heritages)

→ hole punch

→ yarn

INSTRUCTIONS

1. Provide each student with at least four squares of fabric. Punch two holes in each side of the square.

2. Invite each child to use their yarn to match the two holes on their two squares of fabric and connect them by threading the yarn through two of the holes on one side of each of their two squares.

3. Once each child has connected their two fabric squares, move children into groups. Instruct students to work together to connect their pieces to make one quilt.

4. Once the quilt is complete, display it in your classroom.

5. Clean up from the arts and crafts experience and gather the children for closing thoughts and the "ELEVATE! Superstars" song.

We Rise Together

Pause to review the progress for the day or for the week. Reinforce this lesson's key themes with your students, affirming their progress and participation.

Say, "In today's lesson, we were able to use creativity to see something beautiful in things that many people don't see as beautiful or valuable. And now we have worked together to use cooperation and creativity to make something beautiful for our ELEVATE! community."

"ELEVATE! SUPERSTARS"

➡ [Child's name/group name/class name] is a superstar!

➡ [Child's achievement] makes [her/him] a superstar!

➡ Keep shooting for the stars, ELEVATE! superstars!

➡ We love to watch you elevate!

ELEVATING INTO OUR FUTURE

ELEVATE! Focus: Elevating Our Future

You have a bright future. When you dream big and step into your future now and you believe in your future, you elevate yourself, your friends and family, and your community.

ELEVATE! Objective: Demonstrate Vision for the Future

Students will connect to their hope for the future and believe in the power of their dreams for the future. Over time, students will become more confident in embodying their future now.

ELEVATE! Reading: Books for Elevating Our Future

➡ *I Am Albert Einstein* by Brad Meltzer and Christopher Eliopoulos

➡ *Best in Me* by Natalie McDonald-Perkins and Mary Ibeh

➡ *When I Grow Up, I Want to Be a Song!* by Danielle LaRosa and Pardeep Mehra

➡ *Maybe* by Kobi Yamada and Gabriella Barouch

ELEVATE! Family Support: Elevating Our Future

Support the child's experience during this unit of ELEVATE! through encouraging and affirming conversations that focus on hopes and dreams for a bright future. Notice each child's level of clarity and disposition toward his or her future. Speak words of positive affirmation and belief to your child and encourage them to dream big.

When you dream big and step into your future now and you believe in your future, you elevate yourself, your friends and family, and your community.

LESSON 1: JOURNEY TO THE FUTURE

We Shine Together

Say, "Welcome, everyone! Are we ready to *elevate*?" Encourage the children to respond actively and with enthusiasm.

Ask the three daily questions in the ELEVATE! Affirmations section below. You may wish to call on children or simply post the question to the whole group and wait for responses. Invite the children to use their imagination to try new ways to elevate their day and the experience of their classmates.

ELEVATE! AFFIRMATIONS

"Today I feel _____

_____

_____."

"I can make my day better by _____

_____

_____."

"I can help make _____'s day

better by _____

_____

_____."

Remind the children that it's OK to begin where they are. Say, "No matter what kind of day you're having, who you are and how you are is just fine because, together, we can ..." Wait for the children to respond with "Elevate!"

Say, "That's right! Together, we can elevate! Today we'll be talking about how we can elevate our *future*. But first, let's do our ELEVATE! affirmations. I'm going to read each affirmation, and I want to invite *you* to raise your hand if you'd like to share an affirmation today."

Allow three or four responses per question. If time allows, give students time for further reflection and expression, whenever possible focusing on a positive trajectory for their day from here. Ensure that all children are given the opportunity to participate over the course of your after-school program.

"ELEVATE! AFFIRMATION" SONG

Beginning each lesson with the affirmation song allows you, the teacher, to set the cultural tone for the classroom—a tone that tells the students that everyone is welcome and that each and every child will be loved and accepted for their unique traits and abilities. Students can sing along with the recorded version.

Encourage all students to express themselves by singing or participating in a way that feels good to them. You might make instruments available, for example, and encourage the children to clap or snap their fingers to keep the rhythm. If you choose, you may also encourage body movements, such as swaying from side to side, dancing creatively, or jumping on the word *elevate*.

Mathematicians and artists,

Musicians and lyricists,

They are all gifts;

They are loved at ELEVATE!

Athletes and readers,

Supporters and leaders,

All kinds of believers

Are loved at ELEVATE!

Hair kinky or straight,

Long tresses or a fade,

Eyes of all shapes

Are loved at ELEVATE!

Fair skin

To every shade of melanin,

We are all kin;

You are loved at ELEVATE!

A temperament that's mild

Or with a little bit of spice,

Personas of all types

Are loved at ELEVATE!

At ELEVATE!

Everybody can find their place;

Never have to worry about feeling hate.

Everybody's loved at ELEVATE!

We Learn Together

ELEVATE! FOCUS

Introduce the theme of this unit—elevating our future. The ELEVATE! focus in this lesson is journey to the future. Guide the children in the key themes of this lesson using the suggested conversation highlights below.

Say, "Today we're going to learn about the journey into our future. Let's look at some words you've probably heard before in a new way." Introduce each word and guide the discussion using the questions below.

FUTURE

- Have you heard of the word *future*?
- Where have you heard the word *future*?
- Who can put the word *future* in a sentence?
- Can you see your future?
- Can you have dreams for your future?
- Can you make choices that help you reach the future you want?

PURPOSE

- What do you think *purpose* means?
- What does it mean to have purpose?
- Who can put the word *purpose* in a sentence?
- When have you felt a special purpose for doing something?

SPECIAL

➡ Have you ever heard of the word *special*?

➡ Where have you heard the word *special*?

➡ Who can put the word *special* in a sentence?

➡ What do you think *special* means?

CONTRIBUTION

➡ Have you ever heard of the word *contribution*?

➡ Where have you heard the word *contribution*?

➡ Who can put the word *contribution* in a sentence?

➡ What do you think *contribution* means?

Say, "Your purpose is even bigger than a goal. It is your reason for being on this earth. Your purpose is the reason you set certain goals." Discuss purpose, allowing students to share their thoughts, using the following points as a guideline for your discussion.

Why is it important to have a purpose?

➡ When you feel like your life has purpose, you are more likely to set goals and reach them. You are more likely to make positive choices because you don't want anything to stop you from fulfilling your purpose for being here on the earth.

➡ In ELEVATE!, we have spent weeks learning about why you are important, why you are valued, and why *you* are a superstar. Each one of you should feel confident in finding your purpose because you know that you are an ELEVATE! superstar. You know you can live your purpose when you aim *beyond the stars*.

Is it easy to figure out your purpose?

➡ No, but you can start by thinking about those things we talked about in elevating our confidence. We can think about those things that we like to do. We can think about the goals we already set. We can think about how we can use those things we like to do or the things we're good at. We can think about the goals we have set to make our ELEVATE! family special and give our best to lift up our classrooms, our schools, and our communities.

Do you have to be a grown-up to have a purpose?

➡ Let's see. (Share images of Yolanda Renee King, daughter of Martin Luther King III; Naomi Wadler, March for our Lives; and the Birmingham Children's Crusade.)

➡ Are these grown-ups? What does it look like they're doing?

➡ Where do you think they might be?

➡ What do you think one of their goals might be?

➡ What do you think their purpose might be?

ELEVATE! READING CIRCLE

The ELEVATE! curriculum features easy-to-read illustrated books about children from different backgrounds. Each of the recommended books is available online. Place children in age-appropriate small groups. Read the story, then explore the discussion questions, which help measure reading comprehension, enhance understanding of key themes, and engage students with the story and its connection to the theme.

BOOK SELECTION: *I Am Albert Einstein*

➡ If you have enough staff members or volunteers, move the children into small groups for reading time with one adult per group.

➡ Hold up the cover of the book *I Am Albert Einstein* by Brad Meltzer and Christopher Eliopoulos. Ask, "What do you think this story might be about?" Invite responses. Remain curious. Ask students to elaborate on their thoughts.

➡ Ask, "Have you heard the word *fiction*? Who knows what *fiction* means? Have you ever heard the word *nonfiction*?"

➡ Ask, "Who knows what *nonfiction* means? Do you think this story is fiction or nonfiction?"

➡ Read the selected book. Say, "As we read the book, think about which kind of story this might be. Is it fiction or nonfiction?"

We Grow Together

DISCUSSION QUESTIONS: *I Am Albert Einstein*

➡ Who was Albert Einstein?

➡ How did people treat him?

➡ What was different about how Albert thought?

➡ How did Albert spend his spare time?

➡ What began Albert's fascination with science and math?

➡ Did Albert let the opinions of others influence what he thought about himself?

➡ What was Albert's great discovery?

➡ What honor did Albert win?

Say, "In the book *I Am Albert Einstein*, we saw how people who are different are treated. Sometimes when we don't appear to have one type of talent, people can tell us we don't have any talent. What they say or how they treat us might make us think that we don't have any talent or any contributions to make. Though Albert did not speak right away, we learned that his purpose was not to solve questions related to language. Instead, his purpose was to increase our understanding of science and math. So even though Albert's journey wasn't clear at the beginning, the way he experienced barriers in one area helped put him on the journey to his real purpose."

We Strive Together

Lesson plans will include ELEVATE! Wise Words. The Wise Words vocabulary will be connected to the reading lesson designed to build language skills and help students meet Common Core benchmarks. At this point, we continue building on vocabulary and linking it back to the story—in addition to reinforcing phonetic concepts introduced in previous units. Below, the focus is broken down by grade level.

Kindergartners: With prompting and support, be able to ask and answer questions about key details in a text. Be able to ask and answer questions about unknown words in a text.[21]

First Graders: Be able to ask and answer questions about key details in a text and describe characters, settings, and major events in a story using key details.[22]

---

21   Common Core State Standards Initiative, "English Language Arts Standards," accessed September 3, 2021, http://www.corestandards.org/ELA-Literacy/RI/K/1/ and http://www.corestandards.org/ELA-Literacy/RI/K/4/.

22   Ibid., accessed September 3, 2021, http://www.corestandards.org/ELA-Literacy/RL/1/1/ and http://www.corestandards.org/ELA-Literacy/RL/1/3/.

Second Graders: Be able to ask and answer such questions as *who, what, where, when, why*, and *how* to demonstrate understanding of key details in a text.[23]

Third Graders: Be able to describe the overall structure of a story, including describing how the beginning introduces the story and how the ending concludes the action, and be able to describe how characters in a story respond to major events and challenges.[24]

WISE WORDS

General Vocabulary

➡ Purpose

➡ Special

➡ Future

➡ Contribution

➡ Fiction

➡ Nonfiction

I Am Albert Einstein *Vocabulary*

Grades K–1	Grades 2–3	
Born	Never	Universe
Head	Actually	Patience
Giant	Scared	Persistence
Way	Speech	Genius
Weird	Whispering	

---

23   Ibid., accessed September 3, 2021, http://www.corestandards.org/ELA-Literacy/RI/2/1/.

24   Ibid., accessed September 3, 2021, http://www.corestandards.org/ELA-Literacy/RL/3/5/ and http://www.corestandards.org/ELA-Literacy/RL/3/3/.

We Work Together

ELEVATE! ARTS AND CRAFTS

Each lesson will include an arts and crafts project that aligns with the theme of the unit. This will allow students to expand the lesson further and apply and expand upon the new learning through other types of intelligence and experiences. To explore the topic of elevating our future and journey to the future, engage the children in a crafting activity to create an ELEVATE! purpose poster.

Gather the supplies listed below in advance. If you are teaching virtually, adapt the instructions and provide an arts and crafts kit that the parents or caregivers may pick up or that you send home for children.

MATERIALS

➡ Poster board or card stock paper for each child

➡ Stenciled letters

➡ Glue

➡ Scissors

INSTRUCTIONS

1. Cut out pictures of influential figures and add a caption of who each person is. Make these available for students to choose from for their poster.

2. Give each child a piece of poster board. Have students draw a circle at the bottom left corner and a circle at the top right corner. They will later add a drawing inside these circles, so they should not be too small.

3. Next, have students draw a curved arrow going from the circle at the bottom left toward the top right circle. Teachers may need to assist younger children.

4. Each child should trace and cut out letters that say, "Elevating My Purpose" and "Aiming above the Stars." For younger students, the letters can be precut. At the top of their posters, students should glue the phrase "Elevating My Purpose"; and at the bottom of their posters, they may glue "Aiming above the Stars." Alternatively, have children write these phrases. Students should leave their circle empty until the next step.

5. At the bottom left, have students draw a picture of themselves.

6. Ask students, "Who do you want to be like when you grow up? Can you think of someone whom you would like to emulate, maybe someone who works in a profession you like or someone who is doing something you might like to do?"

7. Ask students to draw a picture (or choose from the photos provided) of a person they admire or aspire to be like at the top right corner, enclosed in the circle.

8. Along the arrow, have children write, "My purpose is to _____." Students should fill in the blank with their stated purpose, which is likely similar to the purpose of the person they selected to emulate.

9. Clean up from the arts and crafts experience and gather children for closing thoughts and the "ELEVATE! Superstars" song.

COLLABORATIVE GROUP ACTIVITY

Allow time for each student to share his or her poster. Teachers should work with each child to distinguish the career from the purpose as needed. Teachers should ask questions of the students that prompt them to think about the things they can do now to walk in their desired purpose.

We Rise Together

Pause to review the progress for the day or for the week. Reinforce this lesson's key themes with your students, affirming their progress and participation.

Say, "In today's lesson, we talked about a boy named Albert who was born different. People considered him strange because of that. Now looking back, we can see Albert's purpose and the great contributions he made through math and science. We can learn a lot from Albert. What can we learn? First, to remain focused on what you love. Second, to not see being different as being less than. Instead, we can know that being different allows us to make new contributions. So the next time someone tries to shame you for being different, be sure to remind yourself that the world is waiting on you and your unique contributions."

"ELEVATE! SUPERSTARS"

- ➡ [Child's name/group name/class name] is a superstar!
- ➡ [Child's achievement] makes [her/him] a superstar!
- ➡ Keep shooting for the stars, ELEVATE! superstars!
- ➡ We love to watch you elevate!

ELEVATING HOPE

ELEVATE! Focus: Elevating Hope

Hope is your natural state. When you elevate yourself through an attitude of hope for yourself, for your friends and family, and for your community, you elevate your day-to-day experience and live into a better tomorrow.

ELEVATE! Objective: Demonstrate Hope

Students will experience a sense of hope for their lives and their futures. They will see themselves as agents of hope and change. Over time, students will experience more and more confidence in who they are and will embody the experience of hopefulness.

Students will experience a sense of hope for their lives and their futures.

ELEVATE! Reading: Books for Elevating Hope

- *Harvesting Hope: The Story of Cesar Chavez* by Kathleen Krull and Yuyi Morales

- *I Am Walt Disney (Ordinary People Change the World)* by Brad Meltzer and Christopher Eliopoulos

- *Hope* by Kealy Connor Lonning

- *Of Thee I Sing: A Letter to My Daughters* by Barack Obama

ELEVATE! Family Support: Elevating Hope

Support the child's experience during this unit of ELEVATE! through encouraging and affirming conversations that focus on hope. Notice each child's level of connection to hope for each day and hope for the future. Speak words of positive affirmation, belief, and encouragement to your child.

LESSON 1: BREAKING BARRIERS

We Shine Together

Say, "Welcome, everyone! Are we ready to *elevate*?" Encourage the children to respond actively and with enthusiasm.

Ask the three daily questions in the ELEVATE! Affirmations section below. You may wish to call on children or simply post the question to the whole group and wait for responses. Invite the children to use their imagination to try new ways to elevate their day and the experience of their classmates.

ELEVATE! AFFIRMATIONS

"Today I feel _____

_____

_____."

"I can make my day better by _____

_____

_____."

"I can help make _____'s day

better by _____

_____

_____."

Remind the children that it's OK to begin where they are. Say, "No matter what kind of day you're having, who you are and how you are is just fine because, together, we can ..." Wait for children to respond with "Elevate!"

Say, "That's right! Together, we can elevate! Today we'll be talking about how we can elevate *hope*. But first, let's do our ELEVATE! affirmations. I'm going to read each affirmation, and I want to invite *you* to raise your hand if you'd like to share an affirmation today."

Allow three or four responses per question. If time allows, give students time for further reflection and expression, whenever possible focusing on a positive trajectory for their day from here. Ensure that all children are given the opportunity to participate over the course of your after-school program.

"ELEVATE! AFFIRMATION" SONG

Beginning each lesson with the affirmation song allows you, the teacher, to set the cultural tone for the classroom—a tone that tells the students that everyone is welcome and that each and every child will be loved and accepted for their unique traits and abilities. Students can sing along with the recorded version.

Encourage all students to express themselves by singing or participating in a way that feels good to them. You might make instruments available, for example, and encourage children to clap or snap their fingers to keep the rhythm. If you choose, you may also encourage body movements, such as swaying from side to side, dancing creatively, or jumping on the word *elevate*.

Mathematicians and artists,

Musicians and lyricists,

They are all gifts;

They are loved at ELEVATE!

Athletes and readers,

Supporters and leaders,

All kinds of believers

Are loved at ELEVATE!

Hair kinky or straight,

Long tresses or a fade,

Eyes of all shapes

Are loved at ELEVATE!

Fair skin

To every shade of melanin,

We are all kin;

You are loved at ELEVATE!

A temperament that's mild

Or with a little bit of spice,

Personas of all types

Are loved at ELEVATE!

At ELEVATE!

Everybody can find their place;

Never have to worry about feeling hate.

Everybody's loved at ELEVATE!

We Learn Together

ELEVATE! FOCUS

Introduce the theme of this unit—elevating hope. The ELEVATE! focus in this lesson is breaking barriers. Guide the children in a discussion of these themes using the suggested conversation highlights below.

Say, "Today we're going to learn about breaking barriers. Let's look at some words you've probably heard before in a new way." Introduce each word and guide the discussion using the questions below.

IMPOSSIBLE

➡ Have you ever heard of the word *impossible*?

➡ Where did you hear the word *impossible*?

➡ Who can put the word *impossible* in a sentence?

➡ What do you think the word *impossible* means?

➡ Are there things you think are impossible?

➡ What are the things you think are impossible?

➡ Why do you think these things are impossible to achieve?

HOPE

➡ Have you ever heard of the word *hope*?

➡ Where did you hear the word *hope*?

➡ Who can put the word *hope* in a sentence?

➡ What do you think the word *hope* means?

REPRESENTATION

➡ Have you ever heard of the word *representation*?

➡ Where did you hear the word *representation*?

➡ What do you think the word *representation* means?

SI, SE PUEDE

➡ Have you ever heard of the phrase *si, se puede*?

➡ Where did you hear the phrase *si, se puede*?

➡ What do you think the phrase *si, se puede* means?

Say, "Now we are going to do an activity that shows us how we can find strength through *hope*. Can you help me answer some questions? Fill in the blanks for me with the following sentences." Note: Another adaptation is to display pictures with the question and have the students respond with their red, yellow, or green cards or use thumbs-up, thumbs-down, or thumbs sideways.

➡ When I turn on my television, I usually see people of a different color or gender doing _____.

➡ I usually see people of a different color or gender working _____ types of jobs.

➡ I rarely, if ever, see people of color, people of a different gender, or people with disabilities doing _____.

➡ I rarely, if ever, see people of a different color or gender or people with disabilities working _____ types of jobs.

Say, "I am going to show you pictures or words on the screen that show different types of occupations. Have you ever seen a person of a different color or gender or a person with disability who is a

➡ teacher,

➡ astronaut,

➡ professor,

➡ chef,

➡ rock star, or

➡ police officer?"

Say, "Think about the job you want to do when you grow up. Have you ever seen a person who looks like you or a person of the same gender doing what you want to do?" Wait for responses, then ask, "Do you think it will make it harder for you to be a(n) _____ if you haven't ever seen a person who looks like you doing that job? If you've never seen a/an _____ who is like you and you still plan to do whatever it takes to be a/an _____, then that means you have *hope*."

Say, "Today we're going to read a story about a man who ended up in terrible working conditions because, at the time, his community pushed people who looked like him or who shared his ethnic and cultural heritage into low-paying jobs with low-quality conditions. We're going to read how, through hope and perseverance, he was inspired to make things better and to expand opportunities for farmers everywhere."

ELEVATE! READING CIRCLE

The ELEVATE! curriculum features easy-to-read illustrated books about children from different backgrounds. Each of the recommended books is available online. Place children in age-appropriate small groups. Read the story, then explore the discussion questions, which help measure reading comprehension, enhance understanding of key themes, and engage students with the story and its connection to the theme.

BOOK SELECTION: *Harvesting Hope*

➡ If you have enough staff members or volunteers, move the children into small groups for reading time with one adult per group.

➡ Hold up the cover of the book *Harvesting Hope: The Story of Cesar Chavez* by Kathleen Krull and Yuyi Morales. Ask, "What do you think this story might be about?" Invite responses. Remain curious and ask students to elaborate on their thoughts.

➡ Read the selected book.

We Grow Together

DISCUSSION QUESTIONS: *Harvesting Hope*

➡ How was Cesar's life before he was ten years old?

➡ What happened when he turned ten?

➡ What kinds of barriers did Cesar face? What kind of work did he have to do as a child?

➡ Did his family begin to lose hope of returning to their previous life?

➡ What types of barriers did Cesar face in school?

➡ What sparked hope in Cesar in his early twenties?

➡ How did Cesar use that hope to harvest hope in the people around him?

➡ What skills did Cesar have that allowed him to fight for improved working conditions for himself and the farmworkers he represented?

➡ What was the chant that the protesters used? What did it mean?

Say, "In the book *Harvesting Hope*, we saw an example of how Cesar almost lost all hope because his life was turned upside down. Cesar was a part of a cultural group that had been mistreated and used throughout history for low-paying jobs with terrible working conditions. That created many life barriers for him. But when he thought about the parts of his life that were positive, it gave him the hope and strength to figure out how to create more positive places in his life and in the lives of others. Cesar used his vision of what could be better to harvest hope in others. His hope gave him the strength and courage to become a leader for people like him until they received better working conditions. Cesar is an example of how we harvest hope and break barriers."

We Strive Together

Lesson plans will include ELEVATE! Wise Words. The Wise Words vocabulary will be connected to the reading lesson designed to build language skills and help students meet Common Core benchmarks. Below, the focus is broken down by grade level.

Kindergartners: With prompting and support, compare and contrast the adventures and experiences of characters in familiar stories, name the author and illustrator of a story and define the role of each in telling the story, describe the relationship between illustrations and the text in which they appear (e.g., what person, place, thing, or idea in the text an illustration depicts), and identify the reasons an author gives to support points in a text.[25]

First Graders: The goal for first graders is to use the illustrations and details in a text to describe its key ideas, identify the reasons an author gives to support points in a text, and identify basic similarities and differences between two texts on the same topic (e.g., in illustrations, descriptions, or procedures). Additionally, encourage range of reading and level of text complexity with prompts and support for the student to read informational texts appropriately complex for grade 1 and encourage craft and structure knowledge through the identification of words and phrases in stories or poems that suggest feelings or appeal to the senses.[26]

Second Graders: The goal is to describe how characters in a story respond to major events and challenges and identify the main purpose of a text, including what the author wants to answer, explain, or describe so that by the end of the year they can read and comprehend literature, including stories and poetry, in the grades 2–3 text complexity band proficiently, with scaffolding as needed at the high end of the range.[27]

Third Graders: The goal is to read with sufficient accuracy and fluency to support comprehension, read grade-level text with purpose and understanding, distinguish their own point of view from that of the narrator or of the characters, and determine the meaning of words and phrases as they are used in a text, distinguishing literal from nonliteral language.[28]

---

25   Common Core State Standards Initiative, "English Language Arts Standards," accessed September 3, 2021, http://www.corestandards.org/ELA-Literacy/RL/K/.

26   Ibid., accessed September 3, 2021, http://www.corestandards.org/ELA-Literacy/RL/1/.

27   Ibid., accessed September 3, 2021, http://www.corestandards.org/ELA-Literacy/RL/2/.

28   Ibid., accessed September 3, 2021, http://www.corestandards.org/ELA-Literacy/RL/3/.

WISE WORDS

General Vocabulary

- ➡ Impossible

- ➡ Hope

- ➡ Representation

- ➡ Si, se puede

Harvesting Hope *Vocabulary*

Grades K–1	Grades 2–3
Lush	Vineyards
Workers	Poorly
Paid	Landowners
Fight	Company
Strike	Bullets
Grapes	Joyous
Last	Organized
March	Blisters
	Parade
	National Farmworkers Association

We Work Together

ELEVATE! ARTS AND CRAFTS

Each lesson will include an arts and crafts project that aligns with the theme of the unit. This will allow students to expand the lesson further and apply and expand upon the new learning through other types of intelligence and experiences. To explore the topic of elevating hope and breaking barriers, engage the children in a crafting activity to create ELEVATE! Harvest Hope salads.

Gather the supplies listed below in advance. If you are teaching virtually, adapt the instructions and provide an arts and crafts kit that the parents or caregivers may pick up or that you send home for children.

MATERIALS

- ½ to 1 cup boiled spaghetti for each child
- ½ cucumber
- 4 salad tomatoes
- shredded cheddar cheese
- Italian dressing
- paper plate and paper bowl
- plastic knives for each child
- optional: grilled chicken slices
- optional: black olives

INSTRUCTIONS

1. Students should chop their cucumbers and tomatoes on their paper plates.

2. Once completed, hand each child a bowl of boiled spaghetti noodles to mix in with their cut vegetables. After mixing in the vegetables, students should add shredded cheese, followed by their Italian dressing.

3. Mix thoroughly. Students can enjoy their spaghetti salad.

4. Say, "In today's lesson, we talked about farming. Farming is very important for us. Fresh fruits and vegetables, like the cucumbers and tomatoes in our Harvest Hope salad today, fight off illnesses and help keep us healthy. So instead of mistreating farmers, we need to respect them. We need farmers. As you eat your salad, think of the farmers who planted and harvested these vegetables for our health and well-being. And think of Cesar Chavez, who by not losing hope harvested hope in thousands of people who fought for and won better rights for farmers."

5. Clean up from the arts and crafts experience and gather the children for closing thoughts and the "ELEVATE! Superstars" song.

We Rise Together

Pause to review the progress for the day or for the week. Reinforce this lesson's key themes with your students, affirming their progress and participation.

"ELEVATE! SUPERSTARS"

➡ [Child's name/group name/class name] is a superstar!

➡ [Child's achievement] makes [her/him] a superstar!

➡ Keep shooting for the stars, ELEVATE! superstars!

➡ We love to watch you elevate!

HOW TO SHARE ELEVATE! IN YOUR COMMUNITY

Elevating and Equipping Children for Academic, Social, and Emotional Thriving

We have reached a pivotal point in our society. Systems are in flux. Families are responding to unprecedented challenges. Children, perhaps more than any other group, have been affected at every level—to include their academic, social, and emotional well-being. Elevating the everyday experience and the futures of children from a variety of cultural backgrounds has never been a more critical concern. The children are indeed our future, and they are deserving of the intentional investment of our time and our talents. We, as a society, will be affected by the choices we make in this regard.

The ELEVATE! after-school curriculum was designed specifically to meet the needs of an increasingly diverse student population in urban and suburban communities across the United States and beyond. Its multicultural emphasis is a reflection of the world that children encounter on a day-to-day basis in their families, in their schools, and in their communities. To attempt to address the academic, social, and emotional resilience children need without fully acknowledging and integrating this reality is a perilous path that shortchanges all children.

> ELEVATE! places the honoring and restoration of a child's identity front and center.

Unlike many after-school programs currently available, ELEVATE! places the honoring and restoration of a child's identity front and center with lesson plans that value the unique cultural heritage of each child and support expanded opportunity for all. All of this is accomplished while keeping academic excellence in math and reading, educational enrichment, positive youth development, and family engagement front and center. This proven approach has, at its foundation, a belief that all children are gifted, capable of learning, and capable of succeeding academically and socially.

ELEVATE! equips you with the tools you need to elevate our future by elevating children who come from a diverse array of backgrounds and are, at the same time, wholly and uniquely gifted. By setting high expectations for achievement while motivating and affirming children, you as an ELEVATE! instructor, parent, or volunteer make an invaluable contribution not only to the one child you support but to all children, to your community, and ultimately to our collective future.

A Path to Full Flourishing for Children, Families, Educators, and Communities

Millions of children are growing up in increasingly complex, culturally diverse communities in a time when society is facing unprecedented challenges. Likewise, families and teachers are facing the mounting challenges that come with equipping children to grow and thrive in these environments. ELEVATE! is designed to develop academic, social, and emotional resilience in children. In addition to this core outcome, the after-school curriculum also supports families, enriches communities, and gives elementary educators a new way to serve at a high level and prosper as they engage students and build the character and confidence of the children who will lead our world into the future.

This multicultural after-school curriculum supports students, families, teachers, and the larger community in the following ways. It provides:

FOR CHILDREN

- a path to improved academic performance,
- a path to improved social resilience,
- a path to improved emotional well-being, and
- a path to confidence and self-efficacy;

FOR FAMILIES

- a path to practical support for families living in increasingly complex and culturally diverse communities,

➡ a path to peace of mind for individualized attention tailored to the specific needs of the child or children, and

➡ a path to elevating conversations around education and life thriving between parents and children;

FOR EDUCATORS

➡ a path to vital contribution to children,

➡ a path to vital contribution to the community, and

➡ a path to career thriving by using one's unique gifts;

FOR ORGANIZATIONS AND COMMUNITIES

➡ a path to community enrichment,

➡ a path to growing tomorrow's leaders today, and

➡ a path to increased earning potential.

Taking the Next Step to a Flourishing Future

Elementary educators, school systems, and community-based organizations that are seeking a sustainable solution to after-school and supplementary education for children in urban and suburban settings can learn more about ELEVATE! by signing up for a free introductory webinar. In this free introduction to ELEVATE!, you will receive insights about how you can bring ELEVATE! to your community and make a difference in the lives of children and families in your community.

To ensure accessibility and maximum support, ELEVATE! is offered on a subscription basis. When you sign up for a monthly subscription to ELEVATE!, you also receive a full day of training and consultation to fully equip you to deliver the twenty-eight-week curriculum. We will discuss how to adapt delivery of the curriculum to your specific site and create the full ELEVATE! experience for children, parents, the organization or academic institution sponsoring your after-school program, and the community where you and your students live and work.

When you become a subscriber, you become part of the ELEVATE! community. Along with the seven modules, you will receive updates with any new material or updates to the curriculum. You will also have access to regular, ongoing Q&A sessions to answer any questions and address ways to improve your program performance. We celebrate our ELEVATE! instructors and would love to welcome you to the family of educators around the country who are leading the way, helping guide children today, and creating a community of leaders who will strengthen the fabric of our communities and our world tomorrow.

NOTES

CPSIA information can be obtained
at www.ICGtesting.com
Printed in the USA
JSHW031336180422
25052JS00007B/119